THE FALLACY OF SAVING

A STUDY IN ECONOMICS

THE
FALLACY OF SAVING

A

Study in Economics

BY

JOHN M. ROBERTSON

AUTHOR OF

"MODERN HUMANISTS," "ESSAYS TOWARDS A CRITICAL METHOD," ETC

"Let us not confound the statement that *human* interests are at one with the statement that *class* interests are at one. The latter I believe to be as false as the former is true, and, moreover, to be one of those plausible optimist fallacies against which it especially behoves us in the present day to be on our guard."—
Cairnes

LONDON

SWAN SONNENSCHEIN & CO.

NEW YORK: CHARLES SCRIBNER'S SONS

1892

PREFACE.

—>※<—

THE following essay is an expansion of one written several years ago, and recently read to the Political Economy Circle of the National Liberal Club. The character of the criticism it then met with from some of the most competent members removed any hesitation I might formerly have felt as to the chance of my being right in an argument which will strike most readers at first sight as a strange paradox, and which runs counter not only to the standard authorities, but to the views of many of the younger economists who are supposed to have thrown off the old "orthodoxy." The trained economists of the National Liberal Club, to my thinking, did not really defend the received economic doctrine of saving at all: they defended

something else. And yet, while the received doctrine
stands thus naked to criticism, I find that when a
young economist presses the criticism he is made to
suffer for it by exclusion from educational posts which
are in the gift of adherents of the orthodox view.
Having personally nothing to fear in this way, I feel
the more bound to press the true doctrine, as I regard
it, on public attention. I would preface my exposition, however, with an appeal to the candour and
leniency alike of economic students and general
readers, in consideration of the difficulty which
attends all rectifications of abstract theory, and
efforts at new economic analysis in perhaps a special
degree.

As regards the practical solution propounded in the
Second Part, I wish it to be noted that it is evolved
as a strict economic solution of the problem led up to
in the First, and, though it coincides with some proposals classified as Socialistic, is no *à priori* application of any abstract theory of society, and does not
stand or fall with any such theory. In this connec-

tion I am glad to see that a widening hearing is being
won for the doctrine of a naturalist as distinguished
from an idealist treatment of social problems. This
doctrine has been admirably put by a recent essayist,
whose words I have as much pleasure in quoting as
in endorsing:

"The solution which remains to be considered, and which the
course of the argument has gradually brought into view, is the
doctrine of State-control or State-regulation of industry according to the best ideas and knowledge attainable at the time.
This, in distinction from the others, may be called the political
solution. It is untouched by any of the arguments that have
been fatal to the rest. In essence, it is the doctrine that has
been instinctively acted upon both in ancient and modern
States. When a mistaken industrial policy was pursued in the
past, this was not because the State failed to recognise the limits
of its own general sphere of action, but because it was ignorant
of some particular law of economics. The remedy is not to
exclude as many industrial questions as possible from the sphere
of State-action, but to gain the most accurate knowledge of the
conditions of particular problems, and then to apply it both
negatively and positively, and not simply for the maintenance
of prosperity, but for the transformation of the industrial system itself. This does not imply State-ownership of all capital,
which is the Socialistic solution, but it implies that no limit shall
be recognised to the action of the State upon industry except
the knowledge that action would be injurious to the Common-
wealth. Where there is doubt, there may be action or abstinence

from action, according to the probabilities of the case. At a time like the present, when the industrial system is comparatively plastic, the bias ought to be in favour of action." [1]

That may be taken as the political standpoint of the following treatise.

[1] Art. *Politics and Industry*, by Thomas Whittaker, in *Macmillan's Magazine* for January, 1892.

CONTENTS.

THE FALLACY OF SAVING.

PART I.—THE FALLACY.

CHAPTER I.

THE VOGUE OF THE FALLACY.

THROUGHOUT the bulk of the literature of modern
political economy, down to recent years, there runs
the teaching, explicit or implicit, that the practice of
parsimony by all and sundry is the surest way to
prosperity not only for the savers singly but for the
community to which they belong. We have the
doctrine very plainly stated in the late Professor
Bonamy Price's *Chapters on Practical Political
Economy*:

> "The man who saves, be he prince or peasant, is the bene-
> factor of his country; for it is capital which bestows all neces-
> saries an l all comforts, which rescues population from poverty,
> which sustains and increases their numbers. Nothing can be
> more fatal to the happiness of a people than to bring profit into
> discredit." [1]

---

[1] Second Edition, p. 128.

Here, it will be noted, the economist expresses himself as if all saving were made out of traders' profits : but it is not to be supposed, even if he had not made his advice universal, that he wanted to restrict the practice of saving to the profit-makers. He is repeating a standing economic doctrine, which pronounces all saving by individuals to be a public benefit.

On all.fours with this view, of course, is the opinion that if only people in general would be "thrifty," in the sense of "saving" a good deal of their weekly or annual income, poverty would be sure to lessen proportionately, or even disproportionately. This is implied in Mr. Spencer's censure of the English masses for their "improvidence;" his idea being, not simply that they tend to have more children than they can support, but that by not saving some of their wages all round they as a class throw away some of their bread and butter. For it is assumed, as we shall see in detail, by economists of most schools, that the process of saving *money* means the accumulation of *wealth* in the full sense of the term. Thus we find M. Leroy Beaulieu, a leading French economist, in his recent work on the State, remarking that "a few moments of imprudence," on the part of a speculative legatee, "may be enough to endanger, or even to *destroy*, wealth which it has taken the labour and pain of years, it may be of centuries, to amass."[1] M. Beaulieu is here evidently thinking of mere money accumulations, and the dispersal of such accumulations

---

[1] *The Modern State in Relation to Society and the Individual*, Eng. trans., p. 9.

by bad speculations in stock. Yet even to the ordinary unscientific citizen it must surely be clear enough, on reflection, that all that happens is a passing of "claim to wealth" from one hand to others, and that there is no destruction of anything whatever. The same reflection is set up by various passages in a Utopistic novel—now perhaps forgotten, but displaying a considerable amount of freshness of thought, with a good deal of old prejudice—which was published some nineteen years ago. The novelist, not content with endorsing the capitalistic form of society as morally good, thus discourses on economics :—

"Capital is *stored industry*. As the coal-beds, to which England owed its greatness until their approaching exhaustion" [the novel is an anticipation of *Looking Backward*], "led to the discovery of something more efficient, represented millions of years of stored sun-power, so capital represents the *accumulated toil of ages*." [1]

And again, in a description of a public meeting in the future Jerusalem, we have this :—

"On this platform sat the Committee and a large assemblage of the principal members of the Stock Exchange, the heads of all the great mercantile houses, and the governing chiefs of the Jewish people. It was an assembly representative of the world's wealth of *accumulated industry* and *realised property*." [2]

This is not the writing of a professed economist, but we shall see that it is largely in harmony with

[1] *By and By: An Historical Romance of the Future*, by Edward Maitland, author of *The Pilgrim and the Shrine*, etc., 1873, vol. ii., p. 28.

[2] *Ib.*, p. 186.

the teaching of many professed economists; and it
becomes seriously necessary to prove, though many
readers may see it at once, that the "accumulated
industry" and "realised property" spoken of are
pure chimeras. "Realised property" in this context,
if there is any meaning in words, should be tangible
property—lands, or goods, or bullion, or houses, or
cattle, or valuable objects—and not mere money-
title. No doubt it is customary to speak of a man as
"realising" his property when he sells it for money
and has the price standing at his credit in his bank
account; and it is very suggestive of the gift of mankind for conventional fiction, that a treatment of property which consists in getting instead of it the right to
have certain figures marked on a banker's book should
be called "realising," while the process of exchanging
that right for a house is not so described. But Mr.
Maitland's analogy about coal would be meaningless
if he did not signify by "realised property" something
else than the abstract money credit received for giving away concrete property. His words point to
genuine, useful property, as distinct from even coin
or bullion. But in the nature of the case, such property is not represented by the money wealth of
investors in general. It might be argued to exist in
the case of a railway company; but even there the
main part of the real wealth is the land, which is in
no sense "accumulated industry," and the plant, which
is always wearing away instead of accumulating, and
represents at any given moment the product of a few
years' industry at most. Mr. Maitland had not
learned the lesson, accepted by John Mill from Dr.

Chalmers, that the greater part of the existing wealth
of any nation is produced within the current year, as
is seen in the case of the recuperation of a country
after a war.[1] That, however, is only part of the
blunder. The novelist shows that he knows of the
existence of National Debts, and implies that the
capital of his capitalists largely consists in such
securities. He is thus committed to saying that the
eight hundred millions of English debt, notoriously
owing for old loans spent in processes of *destruction*
of wealth and life, represent so much "accumulated
industry" and "realised property," as coal represents
stored sunlight, capable of yielding so much heat and
energy. This is tolerably absurd; and yet, as we
shall see, it cannot be taken for granted that even
economists will admit as much. Many of them still
reason as if the National Debt represented so much
accumulated product of labour, so much actual
"wealth."

The novelist from whom I have quoted, agreeing
with the mass of the economists in his notion of
capital, if not in his way of expressing it, lays down
one proposition which, as it happens, coincides with
past economic teaching but not with present. "To
tax capital," he says in the passage first above quoted
from, "is to tax wages, which are paid out of capital."
Modern economists have abandoned this view. And yet
it is on the face of it distinctly more plausible, false as it
is, than the formulas about the "accumulated industry"
and "realised property" of investors' money-claims.
"Wages" *are* often "paid" out of "capital." Curiously.

---

[1] Mill's *Principles of Political Economy*, B. 1., Ch. v., Sec. 7.

the economists have abandoned the plausible error
without abandoning a correlative error which is hardly
at all plausible to plain common-sense. They have
all now given up the doctrine of a "wages fund," and
yet most of them continue to speak as if saved
"capital," that is, money-claim, were really a "fund,"
the lessening of which would be a deprivation to the
community at large. Professor Sidgwick in his latest
work, a careful and thoughtful treatise on politics,
says of a graduated income tax that "the serious objection to such a measure lies in the danger of *economic
loss to the whole community caused by checking
accumulation* or driving capital from the country.[1]
This might be supposed to mean something different
from Mr. Maitland's doctrine that money capital is
"accumulated industry;" but Professor Sidgwick
goes on to show that he too really has such an idea.
He speaks again [2] still more explicitly of the motives
that urge men to "produce and accumulate wealth,"
as if saving money from income meant the accumulating of that which is produced; and of the probable
"bad effect"[3] of a heavy tax on inheritances in
"diminishing the inducements of prospective testators
to industry and thrift," as if money thrift were as
truly productive, from the point of view of the
community, as industry. In taking up these positions, as we shall see later, Professor Sidgwick is
really retrograding from a much more rational
position reached by him in his previous treatise on
economics, so that it becomes more and more plainly

---

[1] *The Elements of Politics*, p. 173.   [2] Page 176.
[3] Page 177.

necessary to combat the delusion to which he now gives countenance.

I do not anticipate, however, that the main difficulty for most readers will be over this form of the "saving" fallacy, taken singly. I apprehend that many will readily acquiesce in my thesis that the saving of money from income, and the accumulation of credits, is merely a saving of *claim to wealth;* that such claim is not at all represented by actual wealth of any sort at present prices; that an attempt to exchange the whole mass of money capital or bankers' credits for actual property, movable or tangible, would so immensely raise prices as to prove clearly the abstract nature of the capital in question; and that instead of representing "accumulated industry," the mass of capital is rather a potentiality of producing new wealth by setting in motion *future labour*, an extremely different thing. These propositions, I think, will recommend themselves to most open-minded people who are not already hypnotised by conventional doctrines. Such readers may even, I imagine, be not unready to concede that, if the production of new wealth is thus dependent on saved money capital in the sense only that the proffer of abstract or moral claim to wealth suffices to set labour in motion, then labour may conceivably be set in motion to a much greater extent without the intervention of saved claim-to-wealth at all. At least, it seems pretty obvious that if all the members of a small community agreed to help in production of some sort, doing services all round as seemed best from the common point of view, they might accumulate

durable results of industry, as well as produce a
sufficiency of the more perishable products, to an
indefinite extent, without any individual accumulation of claim to the property and services of the
rest.

But just here the problem may easily be obscured
by the suggestion, offered afresh, that in a competitive
society like ours the claim-to-wealth of the capitalist
represents just that right to accumulated products
which in the imagined commune society would be
held to vest in each member equally. Though it
before seemed clear that the saved claim-to-wealth
was not a saved mass of products at all, it would now
seem less clear. And even if the ordinary economists
did not argue that saved money-claim was saved
products; even if Professor Sidgwick should abandon
his plainly erroneous description of the process of
saving, he and the others might still perplex the
ingenuous student by using the old argument that in
our competitive society it is "capital" (in one sense)
that "feeds" and clothes and houses labour, and
"capital" (in another sense) that "employs" and
"pays" labour; and that accordingly "capital" (in
yet another sense) must needs be saved in great
masses to keep our society going, and the more the
saved capital the better it must be for the workers.
And this is what I call the Fallacy of Saving.

How far the fallacy rests on or is fostered by
shifting definitions of capital, will appear in the
course of our examination of the reigning doctrines.
But it will be well at the outset to take note that
while the term "capital" has in practice tended more

and more to signify in particular not plant or goods, but money-credit or claim on bankers' books, or claim in the shape of debentures, most economists have continued to speak of it in argument as if it strictly signified plant and stock in trade, while tacitly employing the term whenever convenient in the other sense. It is not difficult to confute the "saving" doctrine in terms of the avowed definitions of capital, especially in the case of the earlier economists; but when so confuted the maintainers of the doctrine have only to shift their ground in order to open the discussion afresh. We must accordingly hunt down singly the different conceptions involved.

Equally necessary is it to go warily into the other side of the fallacy, namely, the notion that by abstaining as far as possible from consumption all round, people will promote industry all round. Here again it might seem as if the delusion were too gross to have any wide acceptance. Industry is a matter of supplying markets, and the employing class is always speaking of the importance of finding new markets. Not a few of our wars have been made at their instigation, to the end of forcibly opening such markets. And yet not only the "orthodox economists" but this very employing class habitually reason on the assumption that industry depends for its maintenance on *abstinence from consumption*, that is, the *restriction* of the market demand for goods. They do not merely recommend such abstinence to a limited class as a means of providing for the future by securing a claim over the majority: they urge it on all, and habitually speak as if *everybody* might

restrict consumption without restricting the employment of labour; as if everybody might accumulate
claim over the services of everybody else, and so
secure all round the advantages that are enjoyed by
the few who at present accumulate claim over the
services of the many. This, I say, seems a sufficiently
flagrant delusion; and yet there can be no question
about its vogue. Either the advocates of thrift realise
in their hearts that the principle can only advantage
the few as against the many, and are thus putting
forward as a panacea what they know cannot be a
panacea, or they are sincerely possessed by the delusion I have specified. One comes, of course, to the
latter conclusion. That such a delusion should exist,
is unhappily only too easily explained. Like popular
delusions of all kinds, it rests primarily on an unenlightened self-interest. A man wants to "save" in
order to advantage himself; and when he has gained
his advantage he naturally wants to lay on the less
fortunate the blame of their disadvantage. They
might all, he argues, do as he has done. In the same
way he instinctively wants to believe that in gaining
his advantage he has really been benefiting the rest—
that his saving, his non-consumption, has given them
employment and promoted trade generally. Thus it
comes that a doctrine almost nakedly absurd in a
plain statement becomes the creed of a whole class,
who are able, of course, to fortify their creed by
obscuring the issues, which are numerous and, in de-
signing or misguided hands, complex. A doctrine
thus resting on a strongly-felt self-interest must
obviously be hard to overthrow; and if the overthrow

is to be accomplished at all, it must be by a systematic attack all along the economic line.

I propose then, with a view to final demonstration, to go methodically over the ground, tracking the economic doctrine of Saving step by step as closely as may be in the compass of an essay that shall not be a "great evil." The different forms of the fallacy, as I regard it, are always tending to merge into one another as the argument is pushed against one or another; and only a close analysis can dispose of the entire case. There are some, I hope, who will not refuse to be at that amount of trouble to clear up for themselves a problem which lies at the root of the great sociological issues of our time. For this is not an inquiry into the mere metaphysics of economics, like some very able and indeed intellectually stimulating treatises of recent years, but a practical inquiry in the strictest sense of the term. The fallacy alleged and impugned is a fallacy not merely of speculation but of conduct—a fallacy which must, I think, be rectified in speculation before men will in any numbers make up their minds to rectify it in conduct, and which must be rectified in conduct before our social system can to any satisfying extent be soundly reconstructed.

CHAPTER II.

THE CONTRADICTIONS OF ADAM SMITH.

WE are to examine, then, the standing economic doctrine that "parsimony," or "thrift," or the "saving" of money out of income, conduces to the wellbeing not only of him who practises it, but of the entire community in an industrial country such as ours. The common ground for this belief is sufficiently obvious. It being clear that the individual who "saves money" acquires an advantage over his neighbours who do not, it is at least as natural to prescribe the universal adoption of his plan as it once was to assume that the nation with most gold and silver was the wealthiest nation, seeing that the man with most gold and silver was the wealthiest man. And whereas the rise of modern industry set up conditions that led men to look into and to challenge the notion that much bullion made a country rich, those very conditions at first tended to strengthen the notion that "saving" on the part of individuals really did tend to do so. In Adam Smith, who has done most to establish the belief, the bullion fallacy is rejected, and the doctrine of saving enforced, in the same pages; just as it was in Turgot, whom he so closely followed in time. Smith saw that the accumulation of savings in the hands of bankers in his own

country had, under certain conditions, promoted production alike of food and manufactures; and, anxious
to justify the freeing of industry from all restraints,
he argued that under a free system the natural
tendency of the majority to save money would in-
fallibly secure endless commercial prosperity. But
the argument,[1] in which the wish was father to the
thought, is the most superficial and inconsistent part
of the *Wealth of Nations.*

Smith had a healthy preference for industrious
people over idlers, and his advocacy of saving takes
to a large extent the shape of discrediting outlay
which maintains and multiplies "unproductive"[2]
people, as superfluous domestic servants, rather than
productive artificers. The average spendthrift, he
notes, feeds horses and dogs, idle friends and half-idle
servants; whereas saved money, put in the bank,
goes to employ labourers who create objects of value
in return for what they consume. Thus far, of course,
the statement is perfectly just, save in so far as (*a*)
the question of the desirableness of horses and dogs
as wealth is overlooked, (*b*) the question of idle living
in general is evaded, and (*c*) the question is begged as
to the destination of the money put in the bank. It
does not seem to occur to Smith that it might be
borrowed by a spendthrift. There remains the
general truth that the action of the spendthrift tends
in part to turn activity, in the case of those he employs, in unproductive rather than in productive

[1] B. II. ch. iii.
[2] Thus defined, the term, otherwise objectionable, may be
allowed currency in the present connection.

directions ; and that he who multiplies menials is
tending so far to limit useful industry. But even this
general truth is not studied in its relations to other
facts ; and it is obvious that if it be not proved that
the money put in the bank will secure the employment of labourers who would otherwise be unemployed, the correlative facts of the case may be such
as to destroy the moral force even of the appeal
against employing menials. Let us examine further.

In taking it for granted that the money saved and
invested will of a certainty secure the employment of
labour, Smith was assuming that it is always profitable for producers to extend their production ; since
if this be not so, the money put in the bank will not
always be borrowed. Now, in order that it shall be
always profitable to extend production, we must have
one of two conditions : either (1) a stationary or
nearly stationary population must be always increasing its consumption, or (2) the population must itself
be constantly and rapidly increasing, so that the demand for necessaries is always extending. But the
first of these alternatives is excluded by Smith's own
argument and precept. A constant increase of consumption among a stationary population would mean
the reverse of that parsimony on which he declares
national prosperity to depend. He must therefore
look, for that increasing consumption which shall
make possible the continual increase of production, to
the simple increase in the numbers of the people.
That is to say, the proper and certain destination of
saved capital is mainly the employment of labourers
in producing either such articles as frugal labourers

consume, or things which facilitate the production of
these.

Now, Smith had alleged not only that the majority,
at least of well-to-do people, practised saving, but that
the more they saved the more would industry extend,
because—and here the argument is curiously inverted
—the wants of mankind are insatiable. He was thus
virtually predicating, if anything, the possibility of an
indefinitely rapid increase of population within the
limits of biological possibility (which he knew to be
wide), conditional only on the assiduous "saving of
money" by the majority. This very saving of money
or income, however, had been already defined by
Smith to be in reality a saving of products—an
abstinence from consumption—bringing it about that
the products abstained from were consumed by productive people, employed by the lending of the money
saved. "The consumption is the same, but the consumers are different"—i e., useful labourers instead of
domestics, when the saver was a member of the upper
classes. But when the majority *are* productive
labourers, who are to be the consumers of *their*
savings? Apparently the class of the babe unborn.

Even in laying down his proposition, Smith reveals
the fallacy of his contrast between the spender and
the saver. The spender's "revenue, we shall suppose,
is paid him in money. Had he spent the whole, the
food, clothing, and lodging which the whole could
have purchased, would have been distributed among"
the "idle guests and menial servants." But by his
saving some as capital, "the food, clothing, and
lodging which may be purchased with it, are

necessarily reserved" for the "labourers, manufacturers, and artificers." Now, it is very clear that
in the latter case the process can only continue if the
things produced by the labourers are *bought;* and in
the terms of Smith's doctrine there ought to be
nobody to buy them, save in so far as they represent
mere necessaries for the fresh members of the population. But the spendthrift provides better than any-
body else for this mere consumption of necessaries,
since his guests and servants must eat and will waste,
and he is thus actually facilitating for the saver the
process of profitable production. Further, if there be
a moral objection to his employing servants and feed-
ing idlers, the correction of his conduct would plainly
consist in his *buying different services.* "The consumption is the same." Then, instead of saving, he
has only to *buy* chairs and tables and houses, and
the right people will be fed, inasmuch as the unemployed menials will tend to drift into industry.
This line, we shall find, was later actually taken by
John Mill, without any perception that it is a surrender of the case for parsimony.

Yet again, Smith makes admissions which go to
prove that in the end the saving and the spending
will come to the same thing as regards capital :—

"The effects of misconduct are often the same as those of
prodigality. Every injudicious and unsuccessful project in
agriculture, mines, fisheries, trade, or manufactures, tends in
the same manner to diminish the funds destined for the maintenance of productive labour."

But if the precept of parsimony be generally acted

on, and the saved capital be yet used to employ productive labour, there *must* be unsuccess in many of the projects, and those which succeed will do so by ruining older ones. The excess of goods will not be bought. The extension of capital could not go on as proposed for a year unless the precept of parsimony were disregarded.

As his unmethodical exposition goes on, Smith apparently begins to perceive that a policy of general parsimony would not work so well as he had at first assumed, though his admission is made not by a modification of his general statement, but by fresh statements inconsistent with it. He had spoken slightingly of the idle people; but he had also prescribed a policy which, on the face of the argument, was to tend to multiply idle people. Were his advice generally taken, with the results he had predicted, saving would be carried on more strenuously than ever; and as the assumed motive to saving was the prospect of interest, the result in the terms of the case would be an ever-increasing class of people who lived on interest. Spending being discouraged, while interest continued to come in, families would be "endowed" in increasing numbers. Either these would, in accordance with average tendency, live idly on their interest, or they would develop a new passion for industry, and by production add further to the mountains of savings which, as it was, they were accumulating year by year. If they took the former course, we should have, according to the thesis, the phenomenon of a rapidly and continually increasing idle class in an always increasingly industrious com-

B

munity. If the latter, we should have the no less
remarkable phenomenon of a community in which
production was increasingly in excess of consumption,
the majority always producing more and more, and,
in the terms of the case, *selling their products*, while,
on the same assumptions, the same majority *avoided
buying the increased products*.

If, on the other hand, we took only the case of the
working-classes, ignoring the confusion of the thesis,
the same contradiction would arise. Smith's argument had implied, as we have seen, a constant increase of these classes. But his doctrine of parsimony
in that case must certainly apply to them, since it
asserted the necessity of saving on the part of the
majority, if the prosperity of the country were to be
maintained. The majority of the workers, then,
must save. Now, as we have said, saving, according
to Smith, was to mean a refraining from the consumption of part of the produce. When upper-class
people saved, this abstinence meant that what they
did not cause to be consumed unproductively would
be consumed productively by the workers. But now
the workers were *not wholly to consume even that
which was "saved" for them to consume, such abstinence being their only way of performing the necessary
and profitable act of saving*. At this stage of the
exposition, if not earlier, the reader will perhaps be
disposed to abandon the thread of the argument.
That Smith consciously carried it thus far seems im-
probable. If it could be carried farther, the conception arrived at would be something like this :—That
a wise proletariat would always abstain as far as

possible from consuming what it produced, because the more unconsumed products there were, the better it would be for trade.

The reasonable presumption is, of course, that Smith never clearly saw what his proposition led to, any more than the truth which ought to be substituted for it. In economics as in philosophy he tended to evade fundamental issues, making optimistic assumptions where gaps had to be filled. But his cautious common-sense was always supplying him with some saving lights; and he does actually go on, in his chapter "Of the Accumulation of Capital," to contradict his doctrine as to the ruinousness of spending, and the dependence of prosperity on parsimony. Such contradictions abound in his book. He contradicts himself on rent, on interest, and on money. Thus in this very chapter we have the statement that "the quantity of money .... must, in every country, naturally increase as the value of the annual product increases;" although he had alleged only in the chapter before that the circulating gold and silver of Scotland had suffered a "great diminution" during a period in which the "annual produce of its land and labour" had "evidently been augmented." So now, after asserting that the spendthrift, as such, tends to ruin his country as well as himself, the economist not only concedes that "great nations" are never impoverished by private "prodigality," but intimates that "some modes of expense, however, *seem to contribute more to the growth of public opulence than others.*" Opulence is here understood as something different from capital, for the statement is that only

parsimony adds to capital, while the complete spending of revenue neither increases nor diminishes
capital, though it promotes "public opulence." The
preferable form of expenditure, we now learn, is that
which produces good houses, furniture, and works of
art ; and of this expenditure we are told, further, that
it *"gives maintenance* to a greater number of people
than that which is employed in the most profuse hospitality." Expenditure, then, may give maintenance
to productive labour. The whole previous drift of
the chapter had been to the effect that the expenditure of mere revenue counted for nothing in promoting industry, and that only the increase of capital
by parsimony was of service ; and now it appears
that what the frugal man does by his annual saving,
other men do by their annual outlay. There is thus
no final security even for the doctrine that the man
who spends his capital is "diminishing the funds
destined for the employment of productive labour,"
since his very expenditure may confessedly give rise
to such employment, and those to whom his money
passes may do the same without limit.

So deeply rooted in Smith's mind, however, was
the faith in parsimony, that while admitting that
certain kinds of expenditure tended to "public
opulence," he goes on to point out that, after all, "the
expense which is laid out in durable commodities is
favourable not only to accumulation, but to frugality."
That is to say, when once a man has laid out a good
deal of money on durable things, he may stop short
and begin to "save" without seeming to lack money :
whereas those who have spent mainly on sport and

hospitality rarely have the "courage to reform, till ruin and bankruptcy oblige them." Having spent enough on building and furniture and books and pictures, then, the model man saves his money to put it in the bank. To what end? His durable possessions, we were told, added to public opulence, because the more good houses and furniture are made, the cheaper and more accessible these become. But now he has ceased to call for the production of these things; and yet now it is that the main gain is supposed to accrue. His money is banked, and is lent out to producers. In the terms of the case, these are not the producers of furniture, and books, and pictures, for he [*i.e.* the whole class of frugal men] having ceased to buy these articles, there is so far less and not more demand for them, and therefore there is no temptation to the producers to borrow money for the extension of their business. The producers who borrow must be others. Who are they? Hypothetically, the producers of articles for which there is an increasing demand. And what are these? All over the field of consumption, in the terms of the hypothesis, there is frugality, each man spending as little as may be. The only increase in production, then, will be that positively enforced by the gradual increase of population—every year a little more corn, a few more houses, more clothes, more furniture; but no more than can be helped. Thus, on Smith's own prescription, the increase of production, if there were to be no waste, would be in a few branches of production only, and would be strictly limited by the normal advance in population : whereas his prescription of parsimony was unqualified and unlimited, and implied on the face of it that there were no bounds to the possibility of employing saved money in profitable production. He had laid down a general proposition with no practical regard to its working out in detail : he had given society a quack's nostrum, with no other excuse than the good intentions which equally underlay so much of the economic and political quackery he exposed.

CHAPTER III.

THE final refutation of any error, most men agree, is the showing not merely that it is an error but how it came to be made ; and in the case of Smith's doctrine of parsimony this is not difficult. He lived in an industrial society, with democratic tendencies, just at the time when the habit of investment was admitted to have formed a new and important social stratum. His own income, after his retirement to Kirkcaldy, came from investments; and it is natural that the investor should wish to make out that in promoting his own interests he is promoting those of the community. And not only was he the first to grapple comprehensively with the obscure and complicated economics of industry, but he had the current doctrine of parsimony recommended to him by those very Physiocrats who gave him his best scientific inspiration, and whose fundamental positivism bulks so much more largely in his book than his refutation of their formal fallacies. While the Physiocrats brushed aside the bullion delusion, and went straight enough to primary truth in insisting on the pre-eminent importance of the exploitation of the soil, they seem to have tacitly or expressly accepted the immemorial principle of individual money-saving, without making

any thorough inquiry as to what it was that, in industrial society, was really saved by the owners of
investments. Quesnay, indeed,[1] has a curt *caveat*
against "*des épargnes stériles;*"[2] but in this he
merely condemns the locking-up of coin; and on the
other hand[3] he insists that rise in prices is increase of
national wealth. And the lucid and sagacious Turgot,
ably formulating the conclusions of his school, distinctly identifies individual saving with the national
accumulation of a mass of riches. In the very last
section of his *Réflexions sur la Formation et la Distribution des Richesses* he admits that, "en effet,
presque toutes les épargnes ne se font qu'en argent,"[4]
which is more explicit than the language either of
Smith or of the later Smithians; but the problem
thus acknowledged is simply dismissed with the statement that while "l'accroissement annuel des capitaux
se fait en argent,"[5] "tous les entrepreneurs n'en font
d'autre usage que de le convertir *sur le champ* dans
différentes natures d'effets sur lesquels roule leur
entreprise; ainsi, cette argent rentre dans la circulation, et la plus grand partie des capitaux n'existent
qu'en effets de différentes natures, comme nous l'avons
déjà expliqué plus haut."[6]   Here, in the final sentence

---

[1] *Maxime* 21, *Physiocratie*, p. 17.   [2] "Barren savings."
[3] *Max.* 13.
[4] "In fact, nearly all savings are made only in money."
[5] "The annual increase of capitals is made in money."
[6] "All traders make no other use of it than to convert it
immediately into effects of different kinds, with which they
carry on their business; thus this money re-enters circulation;
and the greater part of capitals only exist as effects of different
kinds, as we have already explained above."

of the treatise, the doctrine of the previous part is suddenly and radically transformed ; and whereas we had been taught (§ 49) to think of a "reserve des *produits* annuels, *accumulés* pour former des capitaux"[1] (which again was modified (§ 60) into "*valeurs* mobiliaires accumulés,"[2] but re-modified (§ 61) into "*richesses* mobiliaires accumulées"[3]), we are now to understand that the process of saving is not really one of accumulation of products or riches at all, but the conversion of money into goods or plant by producers—*i.e.*, saving is fresh production. The matter being thus dropped, the practical teaching of Turgot's treatise remains that of his 80th section, which is to the effect that "l'esprit d'économie dans une nation augmente sans cesse la somme des capitaux ; le luxe tend sans cesse à les détruire"[4]—precisely the position taken up immediately afterwards by Smith.

Thus led by his Physiocrat predecessors—whose faith he held on the points of free trade and the fallacy of the bullion principle — to endorse the popular faith in parsimony, Smith could not conceivably have taken a more advanced view. The problem for his day was not that which we to-day term the industrial : the futility of saving as a basis of national prosperity could not be apparent in a society which had not yet tried free trade ; and the very confidence in liberty which inspired the protest against old restrictions excluded the tendency to

---

[1] "Reserve of annual *products accumulated* to form capitals."
[2] "Accumulated movable *values*."
[3] "Accumulated movable *riches*."
[4] "The spirit of economy in a nation augments unceasingly the sum of capitals ; luxury tends unceasingly to destroy them."

speculate on the difficulties that might arise when
trade was free. To question the principle of parsimony and investment as a permanent provision for
national growth would have been not merely to propose reform, but to challenge the whole social system.
As it was, Smith had the merit of analysing to some
extent the facts of the case. It was something to
have gone the length of the proposition that "that
which is saved is consumed," and that what money
saving partly does is to determine how food should
be consumed—whether employment should be given
to footmen or to workmen. It was much better to
have seen that, after all, "public opulence" is increased
by an expenditure which, instead of simply multiplying a proletariat labouring for its elementary wants,
secures durable and valuable products, and so tends
to raise the general standards of culture and comfort.
It would seem, after this, no great matter to have
recognised that a policy of "public opulence" stood
at least as well justified as one which amassed
"capital." But the fact remains that Smith left his
teaching divided against itself, condemning expenditure while admitting that it might promote public
opulence, and urging non-consumption as tending
to encourage production. What is finally to be said
for him is that every publicist in the century had
similarly failed to reach consistency in the face of the
imbroglio of modern industry. Montesquieu alternately advocated luxury and frugality, freedom of
trade and restriction ;[1] Voltaire now insisted that the

[1] *Esprit des Lois*, vii. 1-7 ; xx. 22. Cp. Blanqui, *Histoire de
l'Economie Politique*, ch. 36.

outlay of the rich must always maintain the poor, and again desired the equalisation of fortunes;[1] and even Hume argues for protection as well as for free trade.[2]

---

[1] *L'Homme aux Quarante Écus; Discours à l'Académie: Défense du Mondain.*

[2] Essays on *Balance of Trade* and *Jealousy of Trade.*

CHAPTER IV.

IF Smith was excusable, however, for failure to see round the developing industrial problem before the French Revolution, the same can hardly be said for the economists who, coming one or two generations after him, failed not only to develop his argument but to profit by the criticism directly brought to bear upon it. In 1804 appeared the Earl of Lauderdale's *Inquiry into the Nature and Origin of Public Wealth,* which was in large part a criticism of Smith's doctrine of parsimony, but which also attacked his dogma of an invariable measure of value and his discrimination between productive and unproductive labour. On Lauderdale's own testimony[1] his arguments, especially as to parsimony, were much assailed in his own country, but were well received in France, Germany, Italy, and America; and in 1819 he is found claiming that even at home his propositions "have gradually gained ground to such a degree that, in most recent publications, they are assumed as undisputed and uncontrovertible." To the reader of to-day this is puzzling; for while

---

[1] Second Ed. 1819. Introd.

certainly Smith's confusions as to value were soon recognised, and his (Physiocratic) division between productive and unproductive work soon modified, it does not appear from the ordinary run of economic literature that his doctrine of parsimony was in any degree departed from by his more influential successors. Mill indeed asserts later[1] that "there is not an opinion more general among mankind than this, that the unproductive expenditure of the rich is necessary to the employment of the poor;" and he points to Sismondi, Malthus, and Chalmers, who had all argued that capital could be advantageously amassed only up to a certain point. But on the other hand, J. B. Say, James Mill, Ricardo, McCulloch, and Senior had all sided with Smith; and these were the writers who substantially formed the orthodox English economics of the century, Malthus and Chalmers having little influence apart from the population question. Doubtless Lauderdale heard chiefly the talk of those who agreed with him; and he would tend to have a good deal of not very valuable support for a reason which probably told heavily against him in many quarters. This was his arguing against the proposed rapid reduction of the National Debt on the score that the resulting sudden application of millions of money to purposes of capital, and the withdrawal of so much revenue from ordinary consumption, would utterly disorganise industry. Nothing could be more certain; but Lauderdale, unhappily, never goes beyond the demonstration of the danger, and has the air of being well pleased to see

---

[1] *Principles of Political Economy*, B. I., ch. v, sec. 3.

the National Debt subsist in full for ever. Such a
point of view might be attractive to the idle classes,
but could never be to the majority ; and Lauderdale's
disappearance from notice is in all probability mainly
due to his having thus ostensibly countered one of
the most natural instincts of a democratic and commercial community.

Nothing, however, could be more just than his
whole criticism of Smith. He accepts Smith's view
of capital, and assumes with him that the process of
saving secures the application to productive purposes,
in the shape largely of plant, of a quantity of food
and energy which would otherwise be turned to consumption relatively unproductive. He then adroitly
turns against the advocates of parsimony that very
argument of analogy from individual practice on
which they relied so much, only making the analogy
genuine instead of spurious. An isolated individual
catering for his own necessities, he points out,[1]
would only waste his wealth and his energy if
he turned to the form of capital more of his
wealth than was needed to perform or supplant his
necessary labour ; and what was true for the *isolated*
individual must be true for the total community.
Lauderdale further lays his finger on the point which
Smith had perceived at a late stage of his exposition,
and which, as we have seen, reduced his teaching to
final contradiction :

"Parsimony does not augment opulence ; it only changes the
direction in which the labour of a community is exerted ; and

[1] Second Ed., p. 208.

unless we adopt an opinion which, in economical reasoning, seems long to have been unconsciously cherished—that capital exclusively forms wealth—we cannot conceal from ourselves that if a society, by parsimony, increases its opulence in capital, it inevitably must diminish its wealth in articles produced for consumption." [1]

Nor did Lauderdale for a moment countenance the upside-down doctrine that it is the idle rich who "maintain" labour: he declared in terms of the Smithian sociology (p. 347) that "the real source of increasing wealth is alone to be found amongst farmers, manufacturers, merchants, whose habits open their eyes to farther means of supplanting the labour they perform or superintend:" [2] and he devotes an unanswerable chapter to refuting the assumption that the total of individual "riches" [3] (= nominal command of wealth) served as a measure of the national wealth. But, whether it was that men would not believe that an earl could be a good economist, or that his opposition to the sinking-fund caused him to be ranked with those who called the National Debt a national blessing, Lauderdale's book passed out of notice in his own country, though his formula of the eight contingencies of value [4] was quoted with ap-

[1] Page 210.
[2] In an earlier passage (p. 194) he puts it that "labour . . . is the great means of increasing wealth." He also points (p. 344) to "inequality of fortune" as the "principal impediment to the increase of public wealth," and strongly condemns (p. 364) all interference with trade.
[3] This distinction between "riches" and "wealth" is of course arbitrary, and is not followed in this essay save in expounding Lauderdale.
[4] Worked out later, independently, in terms of the desires

proval by Ricardo.[1]　J. B. Say dismissed him in a
single flimsy footnote,[2] summing up his thesis in the
unintelligible proposition that " l'accumulation *retire
de la circulation des valeurs qui seraient favorables
à l'industrie*,"[3] and refuting this by saying that " ni
le *capital* productif, ni ses accroissements, ne sont
retirés de la circulation."[4]　Evidently he had not
read the book ; but his bogus refutation would settle
the matter for France.　Blanqui in his bibliography
speaks of the *Inquiry* and the Earl's *Considerations
on the State of the Currency* (1813) as works " encore
estimé aujourd'hui, surtout le dernier, même après les
écrits de Ricardo ;"[5] but McCulloch, who drew on
his learning, does not criticise the *Inquiry* either in
his *Principles* or in his *Literature*, merely insinua-

---

of buyer and seller, by Professor Perry, as cited by Professor
Price (*Practical Political Economy*, 2nd ed., p. 46).

[1] *Principles*, ch. 30.　It is probably needless to point out
here the formal inefficiency of Ricardo's contention, as against
the supply and demand formula of value, that the prices of freely
produced commodities " will ultimately depend, not on the
state of demand or supply, but on the increased or diminished
cost of their production."　Obviously the antithesis is only
verbal, and the proper statement is that cost of production
ultimately regulates supply, price being still a function of
supply and demand, just as where supply is determined by
hazard or by a monopolist's choice.

[2] *Traité d'Economie Politique*, 4ième édit., i. 107.

[3] " Accumulation withdraws from circulation values which
would be favourable to industry."

[4] " Neither productive *capital* nor its augmentations are withdrawn from circulation."

[5] " Still esteemed to-day, especially the latter, even after the
writings of Ricardo."

ting that Brougham disposed of it in the *Edinburgh Review;* and Lauderdale is not so much as named in Cossa's *Guide to the Study of Political Economy,* though Roscher and Böhm-Bawerk cite him with a frequency which testifies to some study. Professor Ingram, again,[1] alludes to him with approbation, but with his usual failure to discern the economic issue.

Brougham's criticism[2] in all probability was a means of discrediting Lauderdale among English economists and Liberals generally,[3] though he not only left the Earl's central position untouched but stole some of his thunder. The critic actually adopted without acknowledgment Lauderdale's effective attack on Smith's discrimination of "productive" and "unproductive" labour, just as he adopted without acknowledgment Say's rebuttal[4] of Smith's assumption (on the lines of the Physiocrats) that only in agriculture did Nature assist men's efforts. These refutations were likely to win acceptance for the article as a whole, put forward

---

[1] *History of Political Economy,* p. 111.

[2] *Edinburgh Review,* July, 1804.

[3] I strongly suspect that Lauderdale's grossly adulatory dedication of his book to the Prince of Wales did something to arouse distrust.

[4] *Traité d'Economie Politique,* 4ième édit. i. 9, 13. The *Traité* was published in 1803. Cairnes (*Essays in Political Economy,* "Bastiat," p. 328) seems to credit Ricardo with originating the argument. John Mill (B. I., ch. i., sec. 2, *note*) thought it originated with his father. But as J. B. Say and McCulloch have shown (*Traité,* i. 13 ; *Principles,* 2nd. ed., pp. 56, 65), it was put forward by Count di Verri last century, and later by Destutt de Tracy. And Lauderdale quotes (p. 109) a passage implying it from an anonymous writer (really Asgill) in 1696.

C

as they were in the reviewer's own person; and for
many readers, no doubt, Lauderdale's book was disposed of by a critique whose strongest points were
really derived from it. The book as a whole is depreciated with every air of omniscient superiority that
an early reviewer could assume. And yet the criticism expressly concedes the main argument of
Lauderdale against Smith :—

"If by accumulation our author means only too great accumulation of stock (that is, a greater aggregation of capital by
parsimony, than can be employed), we have only to deny the
novelty or importance, not certainly to dispute the truth of his
doctrine." [1]

But, as we have seen, the whole drift of Smith's
argument had denied that there could be over-
accumulation of capital ; and that was the prevailing
view among his followers ; so that Brougham was de-
preciating Lauderdale on a ground which his own
party could not honestly take. For the rest, when
he goes on to argue that the undue multiplication of
" capital " by production would be just as bad as its
multiplication by saving, because in the former case
also it could not be " profitably employed," he falls
into complete confusion. Lauderdale was actually
arguing that there were necessary limits to the accumulation of capital—that is, stock devoted to fresh
production—and contending that what was wanted
was not more capital but more consumption. In fine,
Brougham's criticism, marked as it was by his usual
hasty cleverness, as well as his usual egoism, was

---

[1] *Review* as cited, p. 373.

merely that of a lawyer.   It was thus at its best on
questions of plain analogy, where it was not original,
and became insignificant and evasive where the problem became vital and practical.   But that is just the
sort of criticism that commonly serves to put down an
innovating argument among partisans glad to have it
dismissed.

The argument of Malthus, again, would seem to
have missed its mark for a similar reason.   He too
gives a forcible answer to Smith's prescription of
parsimony.   The rationale of the matter he sum-
marises thus:—

"National saving, considered as the means of increased production, is confined within much narrower limits than individual
saving.   While some individuals continue to spend, other individuals may continue to save to a very great extent ; but the
national saving, or the balance of produce above consumption,
in reference to the whole mass of producers and consumers,
must necessarily be limited by the amount which can be advantageously employed in supplying the demand for produce ;
and to create this demand there must be an adequate consumption either among the producers themselves, or other classes of
consumers."[1]

And he passes an irresistible criticism on the incon-
sistency of Smith in asserting, despite his dogma of
parsimony, that "the desire of the conveniences and
ornaments of building, dress, equipage, and household
furniture, seems to have no limit or certain boundary."
Smith's course, he points out, "is to found a doctrine
upon the unlimited desire of mankind to consume ;
then to suppose this desire limited in order to save

---

[1] *Principles of Political Economy*, p. 467 : cp. 486.

capital, and thus completely alter the premises; and
yet still to maintain that the doctrine is true." But
while this criticism was never met, Malthus, like
Lauderdale, passed out of notice as an economist,
presumably because he too lent himself to the cause
of the idle classes. His opposition to the repeal of
the corn laws, bottomed though it avowedly was on
his established doctrine of population, would alone
have gone far to discredit him in the eyes of the trading classes; but he had further the unhappy inspiration (1) to put his case in the proposition that the
most incontestably "unproductive" classes actually
promoted public wealth inasmuch as they were consumers; (2) to argue for consumption by idlers rather
than by workers; and (3) to insist positively that
the National Debt was a condition of public well-
being.[1] Malthus saw further into the social problem

---

[1] It is easy to see that it was not want of good feeling that
made Malthus formulate his views so unluckily. He anxiously
but vainly modified his more unfortunate statements. After
ruinously arguing (p. 472) that a greatly increased consumption
among the workers must greatly increase cost of production, and
so diminish agriculture and commerce, and that therefore the
idlers *must* do the extra consumption, he shifts his position and
puts it (p. 489) that even if the workers might have the power
to consume sufficiently, experience shows they have " not the
will; and it is to supply this will that a body of unproductive
consumers is necessary." And he goes yet further. In the
later redaction of his *Essay* (7th ed., p. 473) he even makes
bold to declare that "it is the diffusion of luxury among the
mass of the people, and not an excess of it in a few, that seems
to me most advantageous both with regard to national wealth
and national happiness." And it is plainly the danger of dis-

than the Free Traders; but unfortunately, in his economics, he read it backwards. The question for him should have been: How could the sum of production be maintained while minimising the idle class? He, however, read it simply thus: What would be the effect on production of annihilating the revenue of the idle class, or of causing them to invest their (nominal) capital otherwise than in State debt? Giving the true answer to this, he went no further, and so figured as an advocate of national indebtedness, putting only a few lukewarm objections against his account of the benefits. Finally, as McCulloch was careful to point out, he was not optimistic about machinery; and only in our own day has economic optimism on that and other matters been effectively discredited.

And Chalmers, in his turn, frustrated himself in a similar fashion. Following Malthus in the main in general economics as he did on the population question, he worked out an independent refutation of the principle of parsimony; and he did not fall into the snare of justifying the National Debt. On the contrary, he advanced a telling economic argument for the payment of war debts out of revenue by extra taxation. But he must needs, on the other hand, not only champion primogeniture for the sake of the "moral and humanising effect" of a resident gentry, but propose[1] that the State should make a "liberal provision in all the branches of the public service"

tress that makes him hesitate (*Principles*, p. 485) even about the slow reduction of the Debt.

On *Political Economy*, p. 572.

whereby all younger sons should have places of a
thousand a year! "We should still have the State
to support the younger branches; yet not by the
violation of its integrity, but by a more severe taxation than our politicians of the present day [1832]
have the courage to impose." Somehow the politicians
of to-day are still more degenerate ; and the reverend
gentleman's heroic politics have sunk his economics.

One and all, the English opponents of the fallacy of
parsimony had contrived to associate their argument
with the doctrine that it was a good thing to multiply
rich idlers; Lauderdale seemingly doing it by mere
reticence ; Malthus and Chalmers doing it more or
less of malice prepense. On the Continent, again,
Sismondi's opposition to machinery seems to have had
a similar effect in discrediting his opposition to the
theory of parsimony. In view of the utter neglect of
Sismondi's wisest and weightiest writing, it would indeed be unwarrantable to assume that he would have
been much more listened to had his practical prescription been different. Perhaps his impeachment of the
life of blind competition was in those days too far
wide of the average moral sense to make converts
under any circumstances. Long before either Carlyle
or Ruskin, and with more sanity and temperance than
either, he insisted in the name of political economy
itself that man lived in society to secure his happiness
and not to produce cotton and buttons at the lowest
possible price.[1] Even in London, he pointed out,[2] the
people had made for themselves public parks, and—

---

[1] *Nouveaux Principes d'Economie Politique*, 2e édit., 1827, ii.
141.   [2] *Ib.*, p. 140.

"les habitants ont senti que l'air pur, la promenade, la jouis-
sance des yeux, *sont aussi des produits*, et que la richesse qui
donne de la santé et du plaisir n'est pas infructueuse." [1]

Misconceived and misrepresented by his friend Say,
he thus [2] summed up his attitude towards industrial-
ism :—

"Seulement j'ai prétendu que la multiplication des produits
était un bien quand elle était demandée, payée, consommée ;
qu'elle était un mal au contraire quand n'étant point demandée,
tout l'espoir du producteur était *d'enlever un consommateur aux
produits d'une industrie rivale.*" . . . . "La conséquence de nos
institutions, de notre législation, ayant été de dépouiller la classe
travaillante de toute propriété et de toute garantie, l'avait en
même temps poussée à un travail désordonné, qui n'était point
en rapport avec la demande ou avec les moyens d'acheter, et qui
aggravait en conséquence sa misère." [3]

The general truth of this was later admitted by Mill,
in his avowal that "hitherto it is questionable if all
the mechanical inventions yet made have lightened

---

[1] "The inhabitants have felt that pure air, free walking, the
pleasure of the eyes, *are also products*, and that the riches which
give health and pleasure are not unfruitful."

[2] *Ib.*, p. 462.

[3] "I have simply contended that the multiplication of products was a good thing when they were demanded, paid for,
consumed ; that, on the other hand, it was an evil when,
not being demanded, the whole hope of the producer was *to
withdraw a consumer from the products of a rival industry.*" . . .
"The upshot of our institutions, of our legislation, having been
to despoil the working-class of all property and of all security,
they were at the same time driven to reckless labour, which was
not correlated with demand or the means of purchase, and which
in consequence aggravated their misery."

the day's toil of any human being."[1]   But even Mill
would not see the force of Sismondi's economic argument against the optimistic positions ; and inasmuch
as that went with an attitude of unscientific hostility
to machinery, as well as with a perfectly scientific
propaganda in favour of forms of consumption which
machinery could not meet, Sismondi's lack of influence
is partly intelligible, even apart from the general
backwardness of sociology and the association of his
doctrine with some of those of Conservatism.   Enough
that whereas the natural optimism of the Free Trade
movement was alone sufficiently hostile to a scientific
recognition of the possibilities of disaster under a free
regimen; and whereas even the doctrine of Malthus on
population tended to be willingly ignored by the
average Free Trader as soon as possible, despite its
acceptance by his economists, the English writers who
challenged optimism had further given fatal grounds
for the belief that they were the friends of the old
order and not of the new.   Commercial opinion went
with the optimists who were visibly democrats as
well as Free Traders, and who endorsed the healthy
moral instinct which formally, however illogically,
condemned idle living.

There was, indeed, an optimism in those days which
had stomach for everything, bar protection; which
was content alike with parsimony, luxury, pressure of
population, and primogeniture.   The robust McCulloch
is the typical optimist of *Laissez-faire*.   Defying
Smith, he was not a whit afraid of spendthrifts: he
endorsed Dudley North's decision that sumptuary

---

[1] B. IV., ch. iv., sec. 2.

laws kept a country poor by checking ambition; and he thought luxury a very good thing, as promoting production.[1] He also held that increase of labour depended on increase of saved capital;[2] but then capital was "formed out of profit."[3] He disposed of the fear of insufficient saving by a Leibnitzian pre-ordained harmony:—"It has been wisely ordered that the principle which prompts to save and amass should be as powerful as it is advantageous."[4] With Smith he decided that there would always be more saving than spending;[5] and, again with Smith, he also maintained on the contrary[6] that nobody ever heard of a want of will to spend. Over-population he showed, with Bishop Sumner,[7] to be the basis of civilisation, even if it did reduce wages;[8] primogeniture promoted energy and benevolence;[9] and even taxation, up to a certain point,[10] stimulated thrift and industry. Gluts, though certainly the results of miscalculation,[11] were at the same time really caused by insufficient production[12] of the things which there was *not* a glut; if there was too much of one thing, it only needed, as M. Say had shown,[13] more of other things to buy it up. *Sic itur ad astra.* Taken all round, McCulloch's optimism is a memorable phenomenon. But it was to be superseded by an optimism a little more sympathetic, a little more discriminating, and, at the same time, a little more preposterous.

[1] *Principles*, 2nd ed., pp. 515-523.

[2] Pages 515-534.	[6] Page 185.	[10] Pages 113-116.
[3] Page 116.	[7] Pages 225-230.	[11] Page 203.
[4] Page 112.	[8] Page 484.	[12] Page 185.
[5] Page 535.	[9] Pages 259-260.	[13] Page 201.

CHAPTER V.

THE ARGUMENT OF J. S. MILL.

I HAVE said that the wish was father to the thought when Adam Smith urged that the man who saved money for investment could not fail to benefit his fellows. No other explanation can suffice for the strange energy of error which inspired John Mill's "Fundamental Propositions Respecting Capital."[1] In so far as that chapter is an explicit statement of the wage fund theory, he of course abandoned it later; but no excision of a subsidiary doctrine can save from decomposition the deplorable tissue of fallacy which he thought fit to dub fundamental. The great defect of Mill's great quality of open-mindedness was always laxity of hold on the parts of a thesis; a laxity which made possible to him strokes of self-contradiction not to be paralleled outside of the works of Mr. Ruskin. His father, on whose strength of conviction some think the son's catholicity an improvement, was incapable of these astonishing self-stultifications—of saying in one section[2] that a socialistic adjustment of work to individual faculty is quite possible, and in the next that the supposition is "almost too chimerical to be reasoned against;" of saying in the proem that the laws of distribution, unlike those of production, are

---

[1] *Principles*, B. I., ch. v.   [2] B. II., ch. i., sec. 3.

"partly of human institution," and in the beginning of the second book that distribution is "a matter of human institution solely." These and other vacillations have been exclaimed against by critics friendly enough to Mill; but nobody, I think, has yet done full justice to the indescribable see-saw of the "Fundamental Propositions." Nobody, perhaps, ever will; there is nothing in non-theological literature to compare with it.

The applications of the idea of capital are prepared for by the previous chapter on capital itself. In the first section of that we learn that "whatever things . . . . are destined to supply productive labour with . . . . requisites, are capital." Then we have the statement that a capitalist who has nothing but iron goods can, by a "mere change of the *destination* of those iron goods, cause labourers to be fed,"—the meaning really being that with a portion of the *proceeds* he can pay wages to extra workpeople. Here, too, we have the proposition that capital exists as such by virtue of the owner's intention to use it as capital, an admission that a nation's capital may fluctuate greatly from day to day; which was already a surrender of the wage-fund theory. Then we have the explanation that "all funds from which the possessor derives an income . . . . are *to him equivalent to capital;*" but what is capital to him is not capital to the nation. And yet, after all, we have this illustration. A capitalist, A., lends on mortgage £10,000 ["*property of the value of* £10,000," is the desperate phrase by which the argument is sought to be bolstered up] to C., a spendthrift landlord, who lays it out on "equipages and entertainments,"—the good old Smithian illustration. Then, when it is spent, A. is "*as rich as before* .... he has a lien on the land, which he *could still sell for*" his £10,000 ; but C. is £10,000 poorer, "*and nobody is richer.*" This, though the nominal command of that £10,000, which was all that A. parted with and all that C. lost, was, in the terms of the case, transferred to other people! Of course nothing even of the "equipages" is left : all "unproductive" spending, doubtless, is "unproductive," but for these arguments you are further to assume that the spending man is an organism who makes a clean sweep of all he buys. In the "fundamental" chapter (§ 5) we definitely learn that not only his equipage but his *furniture* is invariably "destroyed without return."

In the first section of that chapter we have the implicit proposition that when legislators by their laws contrive that any portion of the capital of the country be employed in a new industry, that capital "must have been withdrawn or withheld from some other" industry. This is one contradiction of the previous dictum that capital as such comes into existence when a man decides to use as capital what he might have spent as revenue. But the contradiction is promptly recontradicted in the second section, which assures us that not only can capital increase in productive power, but "increased returns" hold out an "additional temptation to the conversion of funds from an unproductive destination to a productive "— which is another denial of the wage-fund theory. Thus is economics made at once a terror to legislator

who create new industries, and a comfort to civilians
who want them. And yet the legislator in turn is
informed that he may " lay on taxes and employ the
amount productively " ! The reeling intelligence is,
however, supported at this point by the quick adden-
dum that the legislator may " do what is *nearly
equivalent*"—he may tax income or expenditure and
pay off some of the public debt; in which case the
amount paid off will be capital, necessarily to be invested—to produce the goods the investor could no
longer afford to buy.

The first Fundamental Proposition had been " that
industry is limited by capital." In the second section
it is explained that " we are not, however, to infer that
it always reaches that limit. Capital may be tem-
porarily unemployed, as in the case of unsold goods,
or funds that have not yet found an investment.'
That is to say, in the case of the goods, *lack of demand*
for the time limits industry. But this contradiction
must of necessity be contradicted, so in the third section
we attain the conclusion that the " limit of *wealth* "
[which please to read as = industry] "is *never* deficiency
of consumers, but of producers and productive power.
Every addition to capital " [including unsold goods or
money that cannot find an investment] "gives to
labour either additional employment or additional
remuneration." And this how ? The goods remained
unsold ; yes ; " but this is seeing only one half of the
matter." " The whole of what was previously expended in luxuries, by capitalists and landlords, is
distributed among the existing labourers in the form
of additional wages"—that is to say, in employing

labourers to make unsaleable goods, which is so much
more beneficent a process than encouraging the continued employment of those who produce the
"luxuries," now also unsaleable. And if you are not
impressed, you must try and assume, as does Mill
here, that luxuries are made by nobody.

After this the fun grows fast and furious. The
cause at stake being that of saving, it becomes a
fundamental proposition that only by saving can you
have capital. There arises the random hypothesis
that without consuming less, nay, even while consuming more, you may produce still more; but "nevertheless there is here an increase of saving *in the
scientific sense.* Though there is more consumed,
there is also more spared. There is a greater excess
of production over consumption . . . . We must not
allow ourselves to be so much the slaves of words as
to be unable to use the word saving in this sense."
In fact, if you will, there had been no great difference
of doctrine between Smith and Lauderdale.

Two fundamentals being thus secured, we reach a
third—that capital, though saved, is nevertheless
consumed—the formula of Smith. And whereas that
might be too difficult a conception to "the vulgar,"
whose eye follows all savings "into an imaginary
strong-box," we have a further interesting demonstra
tion that what is consumed is saved. As thus. The
spending man, that suicidal materialist, effects "a
consumption, that is to say, a destruction, of wines,
equipages, and furniture." But while the destroyer
has been implacably conducting his daily bonfire,
"the saving person, during the whole time that the

destruction was going on, has had labourers at work repairing it; who are ultimately found to have replaced, with an increase, the equivalent of what has been consumed." The beneficent task of this estimable person is thus the production of fresh wines, equipages, and furniture, for the (so to speak) annihilist spendthrift to destroy. But as it appears on reflection that from this point of view the moral merits of the spender and the saver are not sufficiently differentiated, the economist. candidly admitting that the pabulum of the spendthrift "could not in any case have been applied to the support of labour" (which contemns wines, shuns equipages, and distrusts furniture), proceeds to explain that for a change we may produce something else. Since the wine, furniture, and equipages "continue to be produced as long as there are consumers for them, and are produced in increased quantity to meet an increased demand," why, it is the man who demands things who is really responsible for their being produced. On which comparatively commonplace proposition (which, as we shall see, is in flat contradiction to the fourth Fundamental Proposition) there follow some remarks to the effect that structures not intended for productive purposes, such as Westminster Abbey, sometimes last very long, while it does not pay to make durable factories; a truth set forth not so much to encourage saving, which rather runs to factories, as to show more fully that most things that are saved are consumed.

It is after an interval of agreement, as to taxation, with the original but questionable Chalmers, that we reach Mill's fourth and last Fundamental Proposition

Concerning Capital, "which is, perhaps, oftener overlooked or misconceived than any of the foregoing."
This proposition is that "Demand for commodities is
not demand for labour." That is to say, "The demand for commodities determines in what particular
branch of production the labour and capital shall be
employed; it determines the *direction* of the labour;
but not the more or less of the labour itself, or of the
maintenance or payment of the labour. These depend
on the amount of the capital or other funds directly
devoted to the sustenance and remuneration of labour."
Now, we had previously agreed that there was such a
thing as "*additional temptation* to the conversion of
funds from an unproductive destination to a productive"; and it might be thought that a demand for
more goods would constitute such a temptation; but
we have since changed all that. The task now is to
show that mere fresh demand can never extend industry, since the human faculty of demand is a strictly
limited quantity, though it can perhaps be expanded
when saved capital creates supply. To be sure, there
is an admission at the other end of the book [1] that
"restoration of confidence" may revive trade from
collapse; but we are a long way from that chapter at
present; and the creed of the moment is investment,
not expenditure. If, then, you elect to demand one
thing, you must go without another; and if, perad-
venture, you used to save money and are now minded
to spend it, you still do not call for fresh labour, but
only turn labour from other things to do what you
want. It would follow on this that when, instead of

---

[1] B. III. ch. xiv., sec. 4.

spending your money on products, you lend it to a
manufacturer, there happens just the same thing—
you cause labour to be drawn from one branch to
another. But this altogether too simple equation
would give no special moral encouragement to saving,
so it becomes necessary to substitute for it an extended
process of reasoning, in which, haply, things may come
to look different.

To begin with, then, let us suppose that there is a
demand for velvet, but no capital to make it; then no
velvet will be made. So much for that. The proposition is meaningless, but no matter. Let us sup
pose next that there is plenty of capital but no demand,
then, again, no velvet will be made. But in this case
manufacturers and labourers will either produce something that *is* in demand, "or if there be no other demand, *they themselves have one*, and can produce the
things which they want for their own consumption"
—velvet-makers and others having happily always
this resource in dull times. "*So that* the employment
afforded to labour does not depend on the purchasers,
but on the capital." Q. E. D.!

At this stage it is thoughtfully admitted by Mill,
that if a demand for a commodity suddenly ceases
after it is produced, the capital employed is lost. But
we are not to suppose that this is merely for lack of
demand for the commodity. "The employment which
[the capital] gave to labour is at an end, *not* because
there is no longer a demand, but because there is no
longer a capital." In other words, when you are
shivering, with coals and sticks in your grate which
you have no means of lighting, the trouble is not that

D

you have no paper and matches, but that you have no
fire. The student may here inconsiderately suggest
that if demand set in anew it would create afresh that
evanished capital — but — *revenons à nos moutons.*
" This case does not test the principle. The proper
test is to suppose that the change is gradual and fore-
seen "—in fact, if you will have it so, it *is* perhaps
better not to stop your velvet-buying all at once, lest
by stopping demand you destroy capital and dis-
employ labour. But that is not the point: the point
is saving.

A flood of light being thus already shed on the
subject, we proceed to suppose the case of a consumer
at the parting of the ways, as it were, hesitating
whether to hire bricklayers to build, or " excavators
to dig artificial lakes," or simply to buy velvet and lace,
obeying the fatal bias of the typical spender to these
articles. On one side beams the voluptuous velvet
(we do not dally over the lace) ; on the other beckons
the tawny bricklayer, the more sophisticated lake-
excavator being on second thoughts kept out of sight,
so as not to complicate the problem. Now, observe
the difference. If the consumer casts the fatal die for
velvet, " he does not employ labourers; but *merely*
decides in what kind of work some other person shall
employ them. The consumer *does not with his own
funds pay to the weavers and lacemakers their day's
wages.*" Let there be no mistake about that. And
now suppose after all that he had previously been in
the " habit " of " hiring journeymen bricklayers," and
see the fatal result ! He calls for velvet, but where is
the capital to make it ? Alas ! all old dreams of fresh

savings notwithstanding, the capital can only come
from those concerns which formerly provided food for
the now forsaken bricklayers—such being the natural
and inevitable course of commerce! "There was
capital in existence to do one of two things—to make
the velvet, or to produce necessaries for the journeymen bricklayers, but not to do both." Here, perhaps,
the inquiring mind pauses to raise this problem: If
the capital of the bricklayers' provision-dealers is thus
inevitably transferred to the making of velvet, what
is to become next of the new velvet-makers, to feed
whom there is no capital left, though they are earning
wages? And what if, after all, the bricklayers themselves, taking a leaf from the book of their whilom
grocers and bakers, went to work in the velvet-factory?
The fundamental exposition saith not—though to be
sure we had heard that demand for commodities *did*
transfer labour from one task to another.

Rather we turn to this other pleasing hypothesis.
Suppose the slave of velvet "resolves to discontinue
that expense, and to employ the same annual sum in
hiring bricklayers." Now observe the beneficent
change. The velvet-manufacturer "sets at liberty" a
portion of his capital—he naturally would!—and
whereas the reformed consumer is now employing
bricklayers with one fund, the versatile manufacturer
has a "second fund" free to employ more labour with.
Your velvet-maker is thus ready for whatever may
turn up. So "there is a new employment created for
bricklayers, and a transfer of employment from velvet-
makers to some other labourers, *most probably those
who produce the food and other things which the*

bricklayers consume." To the harmonious adoption
of this view, there are necessary only three concessions.
You have (1) merely to assume, for peace' sake, that
no capital had ever been employed in producing food
for the velvet-makers; (2) you are to blot the dismissed velvet-makers from the book of your re-
membrance; and (3) you are not to go back on old
discussions and ask how the velvet-manufacturer
contrives to "set free" the capital embodied in the
velvet which he cannot sell. With these trifling
adjustments, the argument for hiring bricklayers
versus buying velvet is complete. As for the doctrine
of saving and investment, that must for the present be
left to shift for itself; because there is the drawback
that the mere investor does not pay wages with his
own hands: he only enables other people to pay them
as the merest velvet-buyer might do.

That is to say, Mill's attempt to vindicate the
principle of parsimony has ended in negating it.
Smith counselled us to save money in order to *invest*,
or produce goods for sale. Mill, carrying Smith's
confusion further, ends by counselling us to *spend*
directly in wages, on the score that only by such
expenditure can we really "employ labour." The
argument that "capital is the result of saving" comes
to absolutely nothing, for the money saved to be expended is no more capital than any other money
spent in ordinary course. It is spent without profit.
The statement that saving enriches, and spending im-
poverishes, the individual along with the community,
comes to nothing, for in the end it is sheer spending
that is prescribed.

The upshot of this precious demonstration is worthy of the steps. Desiring to help the working-classes, you have hired them *to make a house you do not want, and which you are not to sell.* You are not to sell it, for the reason for which you were not to buy it. " A demand delayed until the work is completed . . . contributes nothing to the demand for labour ; and that which is so expended is, in all its effects, so far as regards the employment of the labouring classes, a mere nullity." On that ground you did not try to buy a house ready-made, or even to order one ; and would you then encourage anyone else to take the nugatory course which you avoided ? No : there is your house; there are the fed and clothed bricklayers: and if you would continue your beneficent course you have only to set them building another useless house, or, perhaps, for a change, digging an artificial lake. That, too, must be made for no ulterior purpose. There was no outside demand for the house you have built ; if there had been, the bricklayers would have been employed by a builder, without your personal intervention. But " when there is no demand for houses, no houses will be made," so that you yourself had to *make demand for the house you built,* after all that argumentation about the futility of demand. Only, you were to take the work of hiring the men, instead of letting a master-builder hire them for you. And it is to this that the argument for saving and investment comes in the hands of the economist who professes most elaborately to establish it ; the saving and investment are finally to consist in sinking capital in personally employing men to build houses

not destined for consumption. And the whole economic upshot, as has been remarked by Mr. R. S. Moffat,
is to indicate a preference for bricks over velvet.[1]

Nor is this all. I have commented elsewhere[2] on
the fashion in which Mill here keeps out of sight in
his "Fundamental Propositions" what he elsewhere
recognises[3] as a fundamental truth in social affairs—
the impossibility of providing genuine labour or even
food for all, unless there is a restraint on the number
born. He does, indeed, put it[4] that on his plan
workers may always be employed while there is
"food to feed them;" but he does not offer the least
hint that the continuous employment of unskilled
and slightly skilled labour would soon carry population to a point at which there would *not* be food to
feed it. He puts forward his unhappy demonstration

---

[1] *The Economy of Consumption: An Omitted Chapter in
Political Economy*, 1878, p. 90. This able writer, who has produced one of the most original books in recent English economics,
an effective criticism of the parsimony fallacy in general, and
Mill's fallacies in particular, illustrates afresh the strange fatality
which pursues the opponents of the doctrine of universal saving.
Like Malthus and Chalmers, if not like Lauderdale, he undoes
his work by ranking himself on the side of privilege. He can
smile at Chalmers' plan for endowing younger sons; but he himself
arrives (p. 376) at the doctrine that landlords are at once necessary and advantageous, " that rent is inseparable from the duties
of proprietorship; that it is the price paid for the performance
of these duties; and that a rent is thus a part of the natural
cost of production." In the face of this perversity I can but
speculate as to whether I in turn part company somewhere with
scientific politics and universal ethics.

[2] *Modern Humanists*, p. 99.   [3] B. II., ch. xii., sec. 2.
[4] B. I., ch. v., sec. 3.

as if it were a real solution of the industrial problem,
and only takes into account the population difficulty
in another chapter, for the purpose of rebutting the
demands of the Socialists who want *State*-provided
employment for all. *Individually*-provided employment is represented as involving no such drawback.
No doubt he tended to see things differently in his
latter years, but there the old fallacy stands in his
book, unretracted. Like Smith, he went on adding
new views to old without reducing them to agreement; and there is scarcely a proposition in his argument on Saving that is not explicitly gainsaid by
others, in the same chapter or later. Thus, after all
his insistence on the destructiveness of the spendthrift, he adds a footnote admitting that there is a
" compensation, more or less ample," in the fact that
spendthrifts " do not usually succeed in consuming all
they spend " *(sic);* and this note ends with a reference to " that part of the Fourth Book which treats
of the *limiting principle to the accumulation of
capital*"—a principle which he has just been expressly refusing to accept. The upshot is that the
denial stands as part of the Fundamental Propositions,
while the truth is recognised at the other end of the
book; and even the glimpse of the rationale of spending does not prevent a repetition of the dogma of
parsimony in the same note. The confusion is hope-
less

CHAPTER VI.

THE DOCTRINE SINCE MILL.

AFTER the foregoing it matters little that Mill goes on to supply half-a-dozen more self-stultifications on points of detail, admitting now that to manufacturers "a falling off in the demand is a real loss;" and that, after all, "an increased demand for a commodity does really . . . . often *cause a greater employment to be given to labour by the same capital.*" These fresh collapses make the infirmity of the writer a little more abundantly manifest : they cannot heighten the ineptitude of the general argument. And yet that tissue of childish sophistry constitutes to this day the orthodox economic teaching on the subject. Mill's unquestionable good faith, with the contagion of optimism which had bewitched him, sufficed to blind men to the abject absurdity of his reasoning. I cannot agree with the late Professor Jevons that the economics of Ricardo is a substantially unsound system, which, by the help of Mill and his followers, has overridden a substantially sound economics set forth by Malthus and Senior; but I am bound to declare that on this one question of saving fallacy has pushed aside science.[1] So far as economics has been

[1] Jevons himself is on the wrong side. He laid down the doctrine of universal saving in the most absolute terms (*Primer*

studied among us, Mill has been the leading authority
down to the other day ; and the popular Fawcett is a
recapitulation of Mill.

Mr. Leslie Stephen has remarked that " Hitherto it
may be roughly said that the advantages gained [from
the study of political economy] have consisted rather
in clearing away old errors than in discovering new
truths—*so far as these processes can be separated.*" [1]
The latter words are suggestive of an imperfect apprehension on the writer's part of the truth he seeks to
expound ; and the suspicion here set up is more than
justified when, a little farther on, we have from him
this deliverance :—

" Beneath the fallacy of the balance of trade and the identification of money and wealth [2] lay another fallacy, apparently
more transparent, and yet so obstinately persistent that its roots
must clearly strike very deep in the minds of most observers.
The fallacy is that which was made celebrated by Mandeville,
and the complete confutation of which lies in the doctrine—so

of Political Economy, pp. 45, 84-6) without once asking how all
the savings could be profitably applied, though he put it forward (p. 133) as a reason why it was absurd for a nation to
accumulate gold and silver that there is "a loss of *interest* upon
their value." That is itself an old fallacy ; but the doctrine
might have set him reflecting upon the excessive accumulation
of money-credits. In his *Theory of Political Economy*, however,
he exhausted his powers over purely theoretic reforms without
coming in sight of the practical fallacy of saving. In the *Primer*
he appears to follow Cairnes.

[1] *History of English Thought in the Eighteenth Century*, ii., 285.

[2] Mr. Stephen is not clear about the existence of this fallacy,
even in the work quoted from (cp. pp. 287, 289) ; and in a later
composition he almost denies that it ever existed (*Fortnightly
Review*, May, 1880, p. 689).

rarely understood that its complete apprehension is, perhaps, the best test of a sound economist—that demand for commodities is not demand for labour." [1]

Of this doctrine, recognised to be so elusive, Mr. Stephen makes no exposition; and we can only surmise that he adopted his conviction second-hand from his friend Fawcett, who had dutifully taken it from Mill, and who so far outwent his master that, like Cairnes, he declined to give up the wage-fund theory when Mill did, continuing to hold it in its crudest form, however, [2] while Cairnes reduced it to the "arithmetical truism presented as an economic law," which might equally have evoked the derision of Marx.

But an abler economist than Fawcett, the clear and careful Professor Sidgwick, takes the distressing course of avowing that Mill's doctrine of demand for commodities not being demand for labour "is, I believe, perfectly true when properly explained," [3] when, in point of fact, the " proper explanation " in his own hands becomes either a truism or a quibble, as you may happen to regard it. He ends by "granting it to be substantially true that the consumers of luxuries do not ' demand labour ' in Mill's sense, i.e., do not supply the real wages of *the labourers who produce the luxuries*" bought by that particular act of demand. And while on the one hand reducing the "truth" in Mill's laborious argument to this complexion, after stating that Mill's argument in support of his formula "appears to me *to a great extent* sound,"

[1] *Ib.*, p. 297.

[2] *Manual of Political Economy*, B. II., ch. iv.

[3] *Principles of Political Economy*, B. I., ch. v.   Note at end.

he notes: "I think, however, that it is all in form unsatisfactory;" and "I think that a part of the argument—that which compares the effects of a purchase of luxuries in a shop with the employment of labourers to produce luxuries—is *quite erroneously stated.*" What Professor Sidgwick here calls a part of the argument is really its essence. But even if he had exposed Mill's fallacy with that explicitness which his conscientiousness seems to make so difficult to him, it would avail little against the reigning cult. Mill's and Fawcett's are still the current manuals.

The same comment is applicable to the latest and most magistral English treatment of Mill's Fundamental Propositions. In his ripely considered *Principles of Economics*, Professor A. Marshall puts forward a view of Mill's doctrine which, while apparently expressly framed to give the most reasonable sense to his Fundamental Propositions, ends by reducing them to nullity. Professor Marshall admits [1] that the statement that industry is limited by capital is "an awkward and unfortunate sentence;" and in examining it later [2] he says that it "has been applied for many purposes," and that Mill himself "chiefly" used it to show that protective duties cannot increase the total employment of labour. Professor Marshall offers no further defence. "This first Fundamental Proposition of Mill's," he continues, "is closely connected with his fourth, *viz.*, that *Demand for commodities is not demand for labour*, and this again *expresses his meaning badly.*" That is to say, Professor Marshall tries

---

[1] 1st ed., p. 138 ; 2nd ed., p. 133.
[2] 1st ed., pp. 569, 570 ; 2nd ed., pp. 575, 576.

to find a better meaning for Mill's words than he
ostensibly meant to give them.   It is thus suggested :

> " It will be found that in every instance in which he has
> chosen to illustrate the doctrine, his arguments imply, *though he
> does not seem to be aware of it*, that the consumer when passing
> from purchasing commodities to hiring labour, postpones the
> date of his own consumption of the fruits of labour.   It is this
> postponement, this waiting, that in Mill's illustrative instances
> really increases the capital ready to aid and support labour ; and
> therefore increases the effective demand for labour.   And the
> same postponement would have resulted in the same benefit to
> labour if the purchaser had made no change in the mode of his
> expenditure."

Here an attempt is made to minimise the absurdity
of Mill's argument, yet even thus it is admittedly
nugatory.   I have only to add that Professor Marshall, in putting the best form on the fallacy, himself
makes an unwarranted statement.   He gives no proof
for the assertion that the postponement of consumption of what is made "increases the effective demand
for labour."   He too, in turn, has forgotten the "velvet-makers," who in the terms of Mill's case will be
either unemployed or half-employed when the employer finds a falling-off in the demand for his products.   Thus Professor Marshall does not finally take
note of the fundamental fallacy of all four of Mill's
propositions; and the doctrine of saving is left in
command of the field.   Every British student of
economics is still shown the folly of the young noble-
man who bought eighteen waistcoats to help trade,
instead of lending money to the tailor to make unsaleable waistcoats, or lay in superfluous cloth.

And one of the most respected of English economists since Mill, Professor Cairnes, who had the
merit of repudiating the old *laissez-faire* optimism
and dealing frankly with the political side of economics in the light of his knowledge, has stood sted-
fastly to the old faith on saving.

"I take it to be a fundamental and indispensable condition
of all progressive human society, that *by some means or other* a
large aggregate capital available for its requirements should be
provided. Without such a fund, *accumulated from the products*
of past toil, division of labour and continuous industry are impossible ; population cannot attain the degree of density indispensable to civilised existence ; nor can that amount of
leisure from physical toil be secured for any considerable portion of the people which is required for the cultivation of
science and literature." [1]

Professor Cairnes, though here pointing to social
arrangements which might obviously be set up on
other lines than that of money-saving, could not conceive that the special process of "sacrifice" which he
saw in "saving" might be enforced in a socialised
State by mere "benevolence and public spirit," and
accordingly decided on that ground against Socialism.
He was positive that "capital can only be created by
saving," and accordingly declared : "If then the
labourer is to emerge from his present position and
become a sharer in the gains of capital, he must in
the first instance learn to save." [2] That is to say,
there may be universal saving, with gain all round—
the old doctrine in its wildest form. It is nothing to

[1] *Some Leading Principles of Political Economy*, ed. 1884, p.
271.   [2] *Ib.*, p. 287.

the purpose that Cairnes points to the money-claim
wasted annually by the workers on drink ; for if that
money were saved it would do nothing for the distillers' and brewers' men thrown idle. Only fresh
consumption could provide employment for them,
and no provision is made in the argument for such
fresh consumption. Cairnes, with all his sincerity
and aspiration, was but helplessly repeating the old
shibboleth, having done nothing to analyse afresh the
special problem involved. He did, indeed, repudiate
the notion that the idle rich class conferred a public
benefit :—

" It is important, on moral no less than on economic grounds,
to insist upon this, that no public benefit of any kind arises from
the existence of an idle rich class. The wealth accumulated by
their ancestors and others on their behalf, where it is employed
as capital, no doubt helps to sustain industry ; but what they
consume in idleness and luxury is not capital, and helps to sustain nothing but their own unprofitable lives. By all means
they must have their rents and interest, as it is written in the
bond ; but let them take their proper place as drones in the
hive, gorging at a feast to which they have contributed nothing." [1]

Here, however, the moral outburst counts for nothing in view of the economic doctrine ; inasmuch as
Cairnes goes on to insist that the only way to keep
industry going is to reward the drones for their or
their ancestors' act of saving, which he pronounces
all-essential. Naturally, the average man pays little
heed to a diatribe thus countervailed by its author's
own admissions. Cairnes had, indeed, on his own

[1] Page 35.

showing, no right to say that the idle rich "contributed nothing:" he expressly credited them with
"sustaining industry" by their capital. His net prescription thus came to this, that in order to be wholly
admirable, the capitalists had only to go on accumulating capital unceasingly while living as frugally as
possible. It would, on his own principles, avail them
no more to spend money on public objects than to
spend it on private, since industry is only "sustained"
by the productive employment of capital. Thus,
Cairnes's economic advice to his generation, despite
the entire wisdom of such a negative proposition as
that quoted on our title-page, was finally futile,
amounting to the old counsel to produce without consuming, to sell without buying.

As against Cairnes's fling at the idle rich, again, the
other economists of the same succession have haloed
the interest-drawing class with an earned or imputed
sanctification in respect of the "abstinence" which had
to be practised to secure the creation of their capital
to start with. And this, which is the older ethical
sentiment,[1] is naturally the more popular with the
interest-drawing class, who can meet Cairnes's attack

[1] Professor Böhm-Bawerk (*Capital and Interest*, Smart's
trans., B. IV., ch. i., p. 269), following Marx (*Capital*, 1., ch.
xxix., sec. 3), speaks of Senior as the founder of the abstinence
theory. But, as Böhm-Bawerk notes, it was put by Poulett Scrope
(*Principles of Pol. Ec.*, 1833, p. 146) before Senior published his
treatise ; and it was explicitly laid down long before either by
Petty, who described interest as "a reward for forbearing the
use of your own money for a term of time agreed upon " (*Quan-
tulumcumque*, cited by Lauderdale, p. 152). No doubt Senior gave
the doctrine its currency. Cp. Marx, B. I., ch. ix., sec. 3, *note*.

with his own endorsement of the abstinence principle—a conception still so attractive that it finds
favour with Professor Böhm-Bawerk, who, by way of
confuting those who insist that a purely negative act
can count for nothing as an aid to production, skil-
fully cites in support[1] of it the very citation from
Spinoza which Marx[2] employed to show that *any* act
may be regarded as an abstinence from its contrary.
Of course, the common interpretation of Senior is a
trifle less sophisticated, at least in his native land.
Here he has been one of the prophets of saving; and
if some, refusing to endorse Mill's applause, have rejected this formula, even these have let the implied
prescription for conduct go uncontradicted.

In French and German economics, so far as I have
seen, there has been on this point the same prepon-
derance of Smithian dogma, though Rodbertus and
others have called for modifications. Roscher has,
of course, contemplated the problem, but is character-
istically inconclusive. He does indeed make an explicit statement of the necessary limitation of capital.

"It may be seen from the foregoing that the mere saving of
capital, if the nation has to be really enriched thereby, has its
limits . . . As trade becomes more flourishing, smaller stores
answer the same purpose.[3] And no intelligent man can desire
his productive capital increased except up to the limit that he
expects a larger market for his enlarged production."[4]

---

[1] *Positive Theory*, p. 123.   [2] As last cited.
[3] So in English translation, made from 13th German ed. The
passage is not in my copy of the original, 3rd ed., and it seems
unfortunately put.
[4] *Principles of Political Economy*, sec. 221, Lalor's trans.

This, however, does not squarely put the point as to individual money-saving; nor is it definitely put in the following observations :

" If a people were to save all that remained to them over and above their most urgent necessities, they would soon be obliged to seek a wider market in foreign countries ; but they would make no advance whatever in higher culture nor add anything to the gladness of life. On the other hand, if they would not save at all, they would be able to extend their enjoyments only at the expense of their capital and of their future. Yet these two extremes find their correctives in themselves." . . . . " The ideal of progress demands that the increased outlay with increased production should be made only for worthy objects, and chiefly by the rich, while the middle and lower classes should continue to make savings, and thus continue to wipe out differences of fortune." . . . . " That there is, at least, not too much (!) to be feared from the making of too great savings is shown by Hermann, *St. Untersuch.* 371 *et seq.* On the other hand, there is less wealth destroyed by spendthrifts than is generally supposed, for spendthrifts are most frequently cheated by men who make savings themselves (Mill i., 5, 5)."[1]

This somewhat bi-frontal performance is probably the most advanced practical teaching on the subject in German economics. Walcker[2] does indeed speak of capital with some alertness of perception :—

" Die Begriffe Capital und Vermögen verhalten sich ähnlich wie die Begriffe Ertrag und Einkommen. Im Worte Vermögen liegt ein Hinweis auf den oder die Eigenthümer einer Summe (z. B. ein Haus und Werthpapiere) oder eines Organismus von wirthschaftlichen Gütern, während das Wort Capital etwas unpersönliches enthält. Es bezeichnet ein Vermögen oder einen Vermögenstheil in seinen objectiven Beziehungen zur Produc-

---

[1] *Ib.* and *note.*
[2] *Lehrbuch der Nationalökonomie*, 1875, S. 8.

tion, zum Umlauf und zur Consumtion der Güter. In der Regel
geht nur das Vermögen, aber nicht das Capital eines Versch-
wenders oder Bankrotteurs unter ; das letztere geht meist in
andere Hände über."[1]

But a few pages farther on,[2] Dr. Walcker begins to
make it intelligible how abstract conceptions of capital
may be brought into discredit :—

"Das Capital zerfällt, entsprechend seinem Begriff, in folgende
Classen : Landgüter, Grundstücke, Bergwerke, Bodenameliora-
tionen, Bauwerke, Werkzeuge, Maschinen und Geräthe,
Arbeits- und Nutzthiere (resp. Sclaven), Haupt- und Hülfsstoffe,
Unterhaltsmittel, Handelsvorräthe, Geld, körperliche und
geistige Arbeitskraft und immaterielle Capitalien. Zu den
letzteren gehören der Staat, die Cultur eines Volkes *und streng
genommen auch ein gesundes kirchliches Leben, wenn es nicht
unpassend wäre, das Ewige unter eine ökonomische vergängliche
Kategorie zu ziehen.*"[3]

---

[1] "The ideas capital and property relate together similarly with
the ideas proceeds and income. In the word property is implied an allusion to the ownership of a total (*e.g.*, a house and
title-deeds), or an organism of domestic possessions, whereas
the word capital implies something impersonal. It indicates a
property or a portion of property in its objective relation to
production, to circulation, and to consumption of goods. As a
rule, only the property and not the capital of a spendthrift or
bankrupt is destroyed ; the latter mostly passes into other
hands."

[2] S. 14.

[3] "Capital, corresponding to its idea, divides into the following
classes : Landed estates, plots of ground, mines, soil-improve-
ments, buildings, implements, machines and utensils, animals
for labour and use (in a sense, slaves) ; principal and accessory
materials, means of subsistence, stock-in-trade, money, corporal
and mental labour-power, and immaterial capitals. To the

After this it is not wholly disappointing to the
believer in immaterial capital to find Dr. Walcker [1]
making the orthodox declaration :—

"Die alte Irrlehre, dass die Reichen, resp. die Regierungen
Almosen geben, wenn sie *verschwenden*, spukt noch immer. Jede
Luxusausgabe vernichtet ein Capital, welches, productiv ver-
wandt, die Subsistenzmittel des Volkes vermehrt hätte." [2]

Thus, within twenty pages of his statement that, as
a rule, only the property (*Vermögen*) but *not* the
capital of a spendthrift or bankrupt is destroyed, the
latter mostly passing into other hands, Dr. Walcker
affirms, in flat self-contradiction, the old dogma that
"*every* luxurious outlay *annihilates* a capital which,
productively applied, would have increased the means
of subsistence of the people." It is the old fatality.
Especially piquant, in the circumstances, is the old
specification of "luxurious outlay" as a cause of
annihilation of capital. On the same principle, obviously, every outlay whatever would do the same thing;
and all expenditure, and accordingly all consumption,
becomes an evil, to be minimised by the self-denial
of the righteous, prepared thereto by "a sound
spiritual (*kirchliches*) life—if it were not improper to
bring the Eternal under a transient economic category.'

latter belong the State, the culture of a people, *and, strictly
speaking, a sound religious life, if it were not improper to place
the Eternal under a transitory economic category.*"

[1] S. 37.

[2] "The old error, that the rich, or rather the ruling classes, give
bounty when they *squander*, is always cropping up. Every
luxurious expenditure annihilates a capital, which, productively
applied, would have increased the people's means of subsistence.

Only a German can attain to quite such transcendent heights; but on the strictly economic line of the argument, Dr. Walcker is not unrivalled in France. One of the most widely-read manual-makers, M. Joseph Garnier, outdoes Smith in his denunciation of the prodigal and his praise of the saver, arguing explicitly that to spend is to annihilate labour, in terms which imply that all consumption is, at best, a necessary evil, while production is man's mission on earth :—

"Toutes les fois qu'un capital se dissipe, il y a dans quelque coin du monde une quantité équivalente d'industrie, qui s' éteint. Le prodigue qui perd un capital augmente la première année le revenu de ses fournisseurs, souvent peu recommandables, mais il détruit pour les années suivantes le salaire des hommes laborieux dont son revenu eut alimenté le travail "—[1]

would have alimented, that is, in employing them to make goods which it would in the nature of the case be prodigality to buy.

And again :—

" Pour apprécier les funestes effets de la dissipation, il suffit de remarquer qu'une *valeur* épargnée devient une valeur capital dont la *consommation* se renouvelle sans cesse, tandis qu'une *valeur* dissipée ne se consomme qu' une fois "—[2]

---

[1] " Every time that a capital is dissipated, there is in some corner of the world an equivalent quantity of industry which is extinguished. The prodigal who loses a capital increases for the first year the revenue of his caterers, often not very respectable, but he destroys for future years the wages of laborious men whose labour his revenue might have maintained." (*Traité d'Economie Politique*, par Joseph Garnier, 6ième édit., sec. 843.)

[2] " To appreciate the pernicious effects of expenditure, it

the thing saved being here envisaged as value, without any recognition that to multiply value is in no way to feed labouring men. M. Garnier has, probably unintentionally, committed himself to one of the delusions of the Physiocrats.

Helplessly led by McCulloch, M. Garnier goes on to recognise that luxury is after all a relative thing, and not to be condemned in the spirit of the old moralists; and in this view reasons that outlay is to be decided on by each for himself, with a view to the highest kinds of enjoyment; but here the good gentleman pulls himself up to reiterate that

"Il ne faut pas oublier que l'homme économe qui se borne au nécessaire rend, de son côté, des services à la société par la formation d'un capital, d'un instrument de travail, de progrès et d'émancipation physique et intellectuelle "—[1]

that is to say, the thrifty man renders a service to society in consuming only the necessary and causing to be produced the unnecessary, which, we have just been told, it is economically injurious to the community for the individual to buy. So that "progress" is always an economic loss to the community.

Similarly M. Droz inculcates saving in a paragraph in which he unconsciously specifies its bad effects :—

suffices to remark that a saved *value* becomes a capital value of which the *consumption* renews itself without cessation, while a *value* expended is only consumed once." *Id. ib.*

[1] "We must not forget that the thrifty man who limits himself to necessaries renders, on his part, services to society by the formation of a capital, an instrument of labour, of progress, and of physical and moral emancipation." *Id.* sec. 813.

" Il ne faut donc point, dans des vues d'intérêt pour le commerce, déclamer contre la prévoyance et l'épargne.   Ce qui paralyse surtout les capitaux, ce sont les circonstances où, mécontens du présent, inquiets de l'avenir, les hommes industrieux suspendent leurs projets, et même craignent de prêter leurs fonds à ceux qui se montrent plus confians ou plus téméraires.   Alors les capitaux se resserrent, le travail languit, la souffrance devient générale." [1]

That very paralysis of production here described is obviously a consequence of such saving as is being recommended, inasmuch as producers will always produce where there is market demand.   Here it is not even pretended that industry is paralysed by lack of "capital;" and yet the advice to amass more capital is endorsed.   Such is the drift of economic prescription in France as in England, the habit of saving being indeed much more rooted and general in France than here.   There must, I suppose, have been enlightened protest against the delusion in France as there has been in England; but it has counted for nothing, the only visible opposition being that implied in the socialistic movement, which does not specially attack the economic fallacy of saving.   Nay, so thoroughly did the Smithian succession establish the optimistic dogma of the all-sufficiency of saving

---

[1] " We must not then, with a view to helping commerce, declaim against foresight and saving.   What chiefly paralyse capitals are the circumstances in which, discontented with the present, anxious for the future, business men suspend their projects, and even fear to lend their funds to those who show themselves bolder or more confident.   Then capitals are locked up, trade languishes, hardship becomes general." *Economie Politique*, par Joseph Droz, 1854, p. 49.

and investment, that when, a few years ago, a London alderman sought to make out that the Lord Mayor's banquet was "good for trade," the outcry against him was virtually universal. He was ridiculed, not for defending a gross and vulgar form of expenditure as distinguished from worthier forms, but for supposing that any kind of expenditure could help trade half as efficiently as would the act of putting the money in the bank. Smith's saving clause about "public opulence" had disappeared from economic memory, and the argument was pure Bonamy Price—for the newspapers had not room for sophistry on the scale of Mill. Not only the middle-class press but professedly socialist economists[1] hurled at the friendless alderman the information that if he or his colleagues had only put their money in the bank it would have gone to build railways—for it is always railways that are supposed to spring from accumulations. This was at a time when "money" was notoriously abundant and extremely cheap, and when promising concerns, such as brewery companies, could have sold their shares ten times over. If the dogma of investment can thus find an overwhelming majority of devoted adherents at a time when abundance of nominal capital and sluggishness of trade are equally obvious, it is not difficult to understand how it could be believed at times when interest was high and trade brisk.

[1] One of these I understand to have since abandoned his position.

CHAPTER VII.

THE RATIONALE OF CAPITAL—THE FALLACIES—THE
DOCTRINE THAT SUPPLY IS DEMAND—CAPITAL
AND MISPRODUCTION.

IT is easy to see, however, that the vogue of the
Saving fallacy has from the first depended on the
mass of misconceptions set up by applying the word
"capital" to the phenomena of money-saving while
conceiving it in the old sense of saved *products*. We
saw at the outset how profoundly this procedure confused and vitiated the reasoning of Turgot. But it
has been just as potent for evil in orthodox economics
since. Everywhere there is made the monstrous assumption that the money, or rather *claim to money*,
saved annually represents a saving of *products and
means of production* to that amount. In John Mill's
lamentable argument about the bricklayers and the
velvet-makers, we saw him speaking of capital as a
motive-force transferable from one employment to
another totally different. "There was," he says at
one juncture, "capital in existence to do one of two
things—to make the velvet, or to produce necessaries
for the bricklayers, but not to do both." He must
have meant money-credit, or money-claim, which
could be turned from manufactures to agriculture, or
from velvet-making to tailoring and boot-making.

Even in that sense the statement is absurd, for the capital is, in the terms of the case, sunk in machinery, which must be unsaleable. But since the mere payment of wages to the bricklayers would at once enable them to get necessaries, it clearly follows that the capital is merely claim on services, which can be transferred. Yet the same economist, in order to justify saving and vindicate the saver, must needs write in many other passages as if to save capital were to accumulate necessaries of industry, without which it must collapse. So, J. B. Say, even with his eye on matter and motion, speaks habitually of a "productive *fund*," which "renews *itself*;" and, declaring capital to be one of the three agents of production, defined it as being at the same time an "accumulation of values."[1] James Mill, after deciding that "the instruments which aid labour, and the materials on which it is employed, are all that can be correctly included in the idea of capital,"[2] goes on to lay it down that in *this* sense capital is "evidently a result of what is called saving"; when all that is evident in the matter is that *food* capital is such a result—that is, primarily. If it be meant that all industrial actions result from saving because proceeding upon food, it might as well be said that they result from air or water, or health, or rationality. But James Mill[3] proceeds to declare in express terms that "the augmentation of capital *is everywhere exactly in pro-*

---

[1] *Traité*, i. 99, 103, ii. 454. "Un capital n'est point la somme d'argent sous la forme de laquelle il est souvent prété; mais la *valeur* de cet argent" (ii. 455, 456; i. 97).

[2] *Elements of Political Economy*, 3rd ed., p. 17.   [3] Page 20

portion to the degree of saving; in fact, the amount
of that augmentation, annually, is *the same thing with
the amount of savings which are actually made.*"
That is to say, the mass of machinery and tools made
each year for productive purposes, added to the
amount of raw material provided for manufacture, is
identical with that year's savings. And as the economist must have had in his view money or nominal
savings, since he offers no discrimination, and must
have known he would be so understood, we find him
formally landed in the extraordinary hallucination
that the net amount of annual saving, recorded by
the bank totals, always equates exactly with a mass
of tangible " saved " materials. We can only conclude
that, like Smith, he did not realise his proposition
conceptually at all, but was merely carrying on a
verbal demonstration, which could only have continuous significance by a continual change in the values
of his terms. As it stands, it is meaningless. Certainly, James Mill has here made a bold and open
attempt to settle the question of what it is that is
saved by the thrifty, and to face the difficulty about
the saving being made in money—the only frank
attempt, almost, since Turgot. But it is a complete
failure, and his successors manage no better.

Ricardo,[1] in the same way, passes with no attempt
at analysis from concrete capital to capital " employed
in the payment of wages," and, later,[2] speaks without
explanation of bankers " employing a large capital "
in discounting bills. Yet he also speaks[3] of diminu-

---

[1] Ch. i., sec. 4.   [2] Ch. iv.
[3] Chs. ii. viii. *Works,* pp. 41, 87.

tion of capital as diminishing the population and the amount of production clearly meaning diminution of food. He thus implicitly accepts Mill's doctrine. And that fantastic hypothesis is to this day found to be the basis of most economists' doctrine as to increase of capital. Professor Böhm-Bawerk notes that "not long ago Kleinwächter (Schönberg's *Handbuch*, 2nd ed., p. 210) could explain : 'common usage in political economy to-day considers it an essential characteristic of capital that it is a material means of production.'" [1] And Professor Böhm-Bawerk, despite his analytical method and his vigilance, lends himself to this virtual confusion of the facts of ordinary commerce—for it is a confusion to define " capital " as above without express exclusion of the common significance of money-credit. He does, it is true, make a formal division of capital into that used for production and that which yields interest, and he demurs to the refusal to call both forms capital.[2] But still he

---

[1] *Positive Theory of Capital*, Eng. tr., B. I., ch. iv., p. 40, *note*.

[2] " Of recent French writers on the subject," he writes, "Gide (*Principes d'Economie Politique*, Paris, 1884) recognises the two varieties in the conception of capital with a clearness rare even in French literature, and distinguishes them as ' capitaux simplement lucratifs,' and ' capitaux productifs.' ' Les premiers,' he says, ' sont ceux qui rapportent un revenu à une personne ; les seconds sont ceux qui produisent une richesse nouvelle dans le pays ' (p. 148). His only failure is that he would recognise productive capitals alone as true capitals." (*Positive Theory*, as cited.) But this of M. Gide is simply a textual repetition of what was said by Droz as long ago as 1851 : " Les capitaux sont toujours des produits amassés par l'épargne, mais ils n'ont pas tous la même destination. Ceux qu'on emploie à créer de nouvelles richesses sont les plus utiles pour la société. D'autres

speaks of capital in the whole as " a group of products which serve as means to the acquisition of
goods "[1] [= wealth]. " Under this general conception," he adds, " we shall put that of social capital as
narrower conception."[2] And the reason for this definition is found to be substantially the Smithian
tradition.

" Without laying any particular weight on the fact that the historical origin of the word capital indicates a relation to an
acquisition or a gain, and that our reading remains true to this,
it preserves the double relation—the relation to acquisition of
interest on the one side, and to production on the other—which
was imported into the conception of capital by Adam Smith "
[Professor Böhm-Bawerk himself shows, however, that the
beginning was made by Turgot, who did it for the encouragement
of saving], " and since his time has been adopted in scientific
usage."[3]

Now, we have seen that Smith's notion of capital,
as set forth in connection with his fundamental
doctrine of saving, was confused and fallacious to the
last degree ; and it is impossible to see how there
could be any gain to economics from adhering to his
definition of capital, even if we guarded against his

---

rapportent seulement un revenu à leurs possesseurs. . . . [Les
capitaux qui] donnent un revenu et qui multiplient les richesses
de la société. . . . sont les seuls vraiment *productifs*, on pourrait
dire que les autres sont seulement *lucratifs*." (*Economie Politique*, as cited, pp. 47, 48.)

[1] There is some danger of misconception of Böhm-Bawerk's
meaning at times in respect of the use desired to be given to the
English word " goods " by his able translator Mr. Smart. See
Mr. Smart's *Introduction to the Theory of Value*, p. 11.

[2] *Positive Theory*, p. 38.   [3] *Ib.*, p. 39.

confusions. But Professor Böhm-Bawerk does not finally guard against them, for while formally disputing Smith's formula that capital is the result of saving, he only substitutes the formula that it is the result of production *and* saving;[1] he adheres to the doctrine that all capital is material; and he explicitly sets his face against those who recognise how extensively the word means something else :—

"Finally," he says, after discussing the various definitions, "there remain those conceptions which see in capital not a complex of goods, but an abstract quantity hovering over goods, as it were; as, for instance, Kühnast's 'sum of value,' or Macleod's 'circulating power.' I have, generally speaking, a very poor opinion of such idealisations of economic conceptions. They are usually cheap expedients for getting round difficulties."[2]

I will not presume to charge against Professor Böhm-Bawerk the use of cheap expedients, but I do say that he himself is all the while evading a difficulty. He ought to have grappled with Mr. Macleod's exposition (I pass over Kühnast), which he does not. Mr. Macleod is almost the only economist who has expressly recognised as matter of economics the distinction between *jus in rem* and *jus in personam*, concrete property and claim; and he is therefore the clearest in his declaration of the economic bearing of credit. He has laid down, too, the one truly

---

[1] This is the old position of J. B. Say, who differed formally from Turgot and Smith (*Traité*, i., 110-113), after saying with Smith that saving is the "only" means of increasing capitals (p. 103), and that to save values is to turn them from a sterile to a reproductive consumption.

[2] *Ib.*, p. 58.

philosophical definition of capital:—"Any *Economic Quantity* used for the purpose of profit."[1]   This definition, I confidently affirm, will survive Professor Böhm-Bawerk's, if only we substitute "gain" for "profit." It covers a multitude of economic facts which the Professor's definition does not, though he recognises them separately as facts. It goes back (which Professor Böhm-Bawerk's definition does not, though he says so) to the pre-Smithian sense of capital as that money-credit which yields a gain. The Professor has shown[2] that Turgot had partly fixed the material sense on capital before Smith; and it is not difficult to see historically how this came about. They were on the side of home production, but also on that of parsimony, and they gave the "capital" significance rather to the kind of property which was in their day beginning to yield the largest masses of profit, as in the hands of manufacturers, who gave capital the material form. At the end of last century, and in the first half of this, the largest gains were made by traders and manufacturers, and attention was fastened on their plant as the chief or "capital" means of acquiring wealth. In later years, competition has greatly lowered the profits of trade and manufacture, and the multiplication of investments has, in general usage, distinctly tended to give the term capital a significance largely made up of mere money-credit or claim.

---

[1] *Economics for Beginners*, p. 45.   See also the valuable treatise on Capital in his *Dictionary of Political Economy*, where he traces the history of the idea.

[2] Work cited, pp. 24-30.   But on this see Macleod.

And the practical necessity of a reformed definition
is finally proved by the collapse of Böhm-Bawerk's
own. The collapse takes place, according to pre-
cedent, when he deals with the doctrine of saving.
He argues, as we saw Cairnes did, that saving would
be as necessary in a socialistic as in a competitive
community. But his proof shows that what is needed
is not at all saving in the normal sense of the term.

"The method," he says, " would simply be to put a considerable proportion of the national workers to very lengthy processes, whereby the *making* of capital, in the form of intermediate
products, would be very great, and the amount of matured
products in the future would be much increased." [1]

Quite so ; and thus is Cairnes answered. The socialistic State would *make* its "capital"= *plant;* and to
call this process " saving," after recognising its nature,
is to make a confusion of language doubly unwarrantable in view of Böhm-Bawerk's own excuse
for his old-world definition of capital. In regard to
present-day saving, however, he himself supplies the
refutation of his definition of capital, and of his endorsement of the doctrine of saving. He admits that
the undertakers or master-producers "do not decide
at their pleasure" the direction which the national
production takes ; "they follow impulses given by the
prices of products. In the last resort, therefore,
it is not the undertakers who decide the direction of
national production, but the consumers, the ' public.' "
Nothing can be more explicit: here we are fully
delivered from the hallucination of Mill. But note

[1] *Positive Theory,* B. II., ch. v., pp. 113, 114.

how the difficulty as to *general* saving is finally
evaded by Professor Böhm-Bawerk. He allows that
a check of consumption causes loss and hardship, but
argues that the demand for consumption-goods must
not be so great as to take all the labour-power
and leave none for replacing and extending plant.
Therefore, so much (of what ?) must be "saved" as
will employ labour in doing this. Now, it is a matter
of fact that in ordinary commerce the replacement of
plant is an ordinary charge on a business, and is nor-
mally met by the plant-owners themselves, leaving
only extensions of plant to be met by outside
"savings." In any case the replacement and extension of plant is clearly a charge strictly limited by
the state of consumption, and represents just that
amount of "saving" or "capital-making" that is
argued for by Lauderdale in opposition to Smith's
doctrine of unlimited saving. Yet Böhm-Bawerk
does not once put this explicitly. The necessary
savings, he declares,[1] "will be spent in the increasing
of capital," because—

"An economically advanced people does not hoard, but *puts
out what it saves, in the purchase of valuable paper, in deposits
in a bank or savings bank, in loan securities*, etc. In these ways
the amount saved" (no limitation) "becomes part of productive
credit ; it increases the *purchasing power* of producers for productive purposes ; it is thus the *cause of an extra demand* for
means of production or intermediate products ; and this, in the
last resort, induces those who have the regulation of undertakings to invest the productive powers at their disposal in these
intermediate products."

---

[1] Page 115.

Here we have one of the abstract formulas before rejected. What is *saved* is here just *purchasing power*. Either this saving is capital or it is not. If not, Böhm-Bawerk's argument collapses to insignificance. If yes, his definition of capital has broken down. And this last is what really happens. As regards the general problem of individual saving, he has passed it by. It is clear that saving in excess of the purchasing power needed to cause the making of plant or intermediate goods *enough for the industrial situation*, can have no producing influence, there being only a given amount of demand for consumption products; but Böhm-Bawerk does not say so. What he *proves* gives no economic countenance to the doctrine of general saving; yet his general language has the air of giving such countenance, and he never undeceives his readers. In view of the clear collapse of his definition of capital, we can only conclude that he had not seen what the problem really was. His further paragraphs [1] are perfectly irrelevant to it, as he simply proves over again that if the demand for consumption-goods were so great that all existing labour-power went to producing them, the stock of " capital," = plant and intermediate goods, would fall off with disastrous results. This obviously impossible conjuncture figures as a final implicit justification of the practice of money-saving in general.

Old sensations revive when we find Professor Böhm-Bawerk after this performance going on to explain with serious unction that in his foregoing exposition he has " risked being tedious rather than being suspected

---

[1] Pages 116, 117.

of sophistry." I will not accuse the Professor of
sophistry save in the sense of paralogism. But I
affirm that he does substantially what Smith and
Mill did in their turn—go astray over one of the
greatest of the practical issues of European economics;
and I can only offer the old explanation, that he was
dominated by a desire to justify the prevailing social
ideal and practice. Fortunately, he being the later
and the closer reasoner, his argument contains the
larger measure of sound statement, and the less
measure of unsound. His practical fallacy is an
implication rather than a statement; and he shows
consciousness enough of his exigencies to make it
likely that his exposition will yet be recast. In the
next chapter he writes [1] with significant heat :—

" If anyone is stupid enough to interpret the theory of saving
as meaning that *finished* capital in *its form* of *concrete* capital
must be ' saved,' he must submit to the retort that man cannot
eat iron machines. But that is not at all the meaning of any
thoughtful representative of the theory. What is maintained
is only that, without saving, capital cannot be made or increased ; that saving is as indispensable a condition of the
formation of capital as labour. And this is literally correct."

What is here called stupid is the express doctrine
of the apostolic succession of economists, who say
that it is products that are " saved." Those who
have said otherwise have been those who, like J. B.
Say and Mr. Macleod, recognise capital as an abstract.
And Böhm-Bawerk, as we saw, has himself explicitly
defined capital as consisting in concretes, and has

---

expressly depreciated other definitions as evasions of difficulties. Now he implicitly admits that capital may have a non-concrete form. Yet all the while he evades plainly answering the general question,— *What is saved?* His case of the socialistic community, however, gives the simple answer. It is *industrial motive* or *inducement* (in our society, *claim to wealth* or *purchasing power*) that is needed to make labour do anything, and "saving," properly so-called, is only our special blind competitionist form of accumulation of such power or motive, an accumulation always defeating itself by misdirection. So that the doctrine of universal thrift is once more seen to be a futility, and the old definition of capital a stumbling-block, on the line of the latest economic analysis.

And yet the ruck of the economists, as of the politicians, mostly adhere to the Smithian conception, vitiated as it is by the flagrant fallacies of its application. Knowing that the claims of investors in national debts are constantly reckoned as capital, they persist in talking of all capital as consisting in material things.

On such a foundation, error is sure to arise. Even Mr. Macleod, who sees that *rights* are economic quantities, and as such, like other credit, may be capital, does not recognise the Fallacy of Saving as it pervades our economics. And if Mr. Macleod misses the practical or sociological upshot, the more orthodox economists do worse. Just as some assume all banked credits to be represented by actual money, despite the notoriety of the fact that they cannot be, so do others assume all credits to be represented by saved products despite the obvious fact that they cannot be. Professor Sidgwick, rightly deciding (though he has since gone back on his perception) that "the greater part of the 'unequalled loan fund' of Lombard Street can never emerge from the immaterial condition of bankers' liabilities," points out that

" this obvious truth is overlooked, or even implicitly denied, not merely in all formal definitions of money, but in most of what is said and written about the functions of bankers. Mill, for instance, implies over and over again that the medium for exchange, which it is the business of bankers to collect from private individuals and lend to traders, consists altogether of coined metal—or at least of coin and paper substitutes for coin made legal tender by Government. A similar implication is contained in much of Bagehot's language. And indeed I hardly know a single English writer on the subject, with the exception of Mr. Macleod, who does not continually present this view to his readers." [1]

But if it be a serious blunder to conceive of all bank credits as being represented by money in the ordinary sense of the term, it is an immensely more serious blunder to conceive of all such credits as being represented by saved goods. Says Mr. Macleod:—

" It is a very prevalent opinion, even among men of business, that real bills are essentially safe, because they arise out of real transactions, and always represent property. But . . . . we have seen that in the most legitimate course of business there will generally be two or three bills afloat arising out of the

---

[1] *Principles of Political Economy*, 1883, pp. 236, 237. Let the reader note how distinctly the admission made here conflicts with the teaching in the *Elements of Politics*, cited in our first chapter.

transfers of any given goods ; so that, in the ordinary course of
business, there will be twice as many bills afloat as there is property to which they refer." [1]

What is true of bills is equally true of the mass of
credits in general. The added ciphers of the bankers'
books represent no addition of "saved products" to
the store of such products available for the "maintenance of industry," but simply the metaphysical fact of
so much general "claim to wealth," claim of which the
validity is constantly fluctuating, being plainly dependent on the extent to which individual claims are
at any moment sought to be realised, relatively to the
state of production. It ought to need no demonstration
that if the purchasing power of money is a fluctuant,
much more so is the wealth-claiming power of credits,
which are but claims to money. In our industrial
system, services are rendered only for the reward of a
lien over other services, and this lien is in the last
resort represented by money. While, however, we
wish to accumulate our claim on services in general,
we cannot all accumulate it in money, and so it comes

[1] *The Theory of Credit*, 1890, vol. ii., pt. i. p. 344. Mr.
Sidgwick, in acknowledging his obligations to Mr. Macleod, adds:
" I must guard myself against being understood to approve of
Mr. Macleod's general treatment of Economics." I regret that
in making similar acknowledgments I must make the same
qualification. In the passage I have quoted, Mr. Macleod lays
his finger on a great delusion, profoundly affecting economic
science ; further on (pp. 481-6) he does desperate battle against
the mere verbal solecism of calling the National Debt a mortgage
on the property of the country instead of a charge on its income.
A reader is invited to suppose that these issues are of equal or
similar practical importance.

to be stored up in simple credits. Thus the nominal mass of saved capital represents simply *claims to wealth* or *power to buy services*, and, so far from the wealth being actually saved, it is in large part purely prospective, for the services which are to constitute it have not yet been rendered. As the National Debt burdens in advance the industry of the future, so does all saving of conventionally recognised claim to wealth constitute a lien over future labour.

The recognition of these simple truths would rid economics of two correlative dogmas which stand in the way of all scientific reconstruction of the social system. The first is that, but for assiduous "saving" of claim to wealth, industry would collapse: the second, that multiplication of "saved" claim to wealth means increase of national wealth.

I. The fear of decline of industry through defect of "capital," in the sense of bankers' liabilities, would be annihilated by the perception that "credit is capital" in precisely the sense in which "savings are capital." Professor Sidgwick's fear of the explicit makes him give only a half-confident exposition of this truth. Mill, he notes,

"speaks contemptuously of an ' extension of credit being talked of . . . . as if credit actually were capital,' whereas it is only ' permission to use the capital of another person.' Now, in a certain rather strained way, we might say this of gold coin : its function is to ' permit' or enable its owner to obtain and use other wealth. And it is only in this sense that Mill's statement is true of the credit or liabilities which a banker lends to his customers, whether in the form of notes, or under the rather misleading name of ' deposits.' This credit, no doubt, is a comparatively fragile and perishable instrument for transferring wealth ; but that is no reason for ignoring the fact that, in a modern industrial community, it is the instrument mainly used for this important purpose." [1]

All this should have been put as emphatically as it is put gingerly. The function of gold coin *is* precisely, and in no strained sense, to permit its holder to obtain and use other wealth ; [2] and on the definition of capital which Mill employed in common with his predecessors, all money is simply permission or title to use capital. Having seen this even partially, Professor Sidgwick has "fallen from light" to Mill's own level of error when in his later work, before cited, he teaches that unchecked accumulation of savings is necessary to the industrial well-being of the whole community. It lies on the face of the argument before us that the power wanted is set up by simple extension of credit. And here is the whole case in a nutshell: that whereas actual money = "capital" means power to get and move products, so credit or recognised title to money means primarily power to get and move money. In practice this latter motion might actually take place, and to some extent does take place, the circulating rate of money being indefinitely capable of quickening; but since the movement of coin can in many cases be dispensed with, the movement of products which brings about fresh production takes place in great measure on the

---

[1] As cited, p. 239.
[2] This is expressly stated even by Mill, B. III., ch. vii., sec. 3. Cp. Macleod, *Economics for Beginners*, p. 33.

simple "permit" of credit, as represented by bankers' liabilities.

But if "faith in the bank" can admit of the movement of products and money, and thus of fresh production, so, obviously, can mere mutual faith as among producers. This is implicitly admitted by economists, such as Mill and Professor Marshall,[1] who maintain, with whatever ambiguity of meaning, that all industry depends on capital, and that all capital is saved. Professor Marshall, we have seen, deprecates Mill's formula in his latest work; but in another passage he still gives it a virtual endorsement in the sense which it properly carries. Bowing, with his usual candour, to the necessity for a widened definition of capital, he includes in individual capital "all wealth or command over wealth which is lent out at interest, whether in money or in any other form."[2] Yet he still states in a footnote[3] that "whatever definition of capital we take, it will be found to be true that a general increase of capital *augments the demand for labour* and raises wages." He adds that

---

[1] Mill's *Principles*, B. III., ch. xiv., sec. 4 ; *Economics of Industry*, B. III., ch. i., sec. 4. Mill, in the passage cited, expressly argues that a commercial crisis is the effect, not of over-production, but of "an excess of speculative purchases." Yet he prescribes new purchases as the cure. Mr. and Mrs. Marshall, while affirming that all supply is demand, explain that " though men have the power to purchase they may not choose to use it," which by context means, if anything, that the error lies in checking their production, which might go on multiplying for ever. And still no word of consumption.

[2] 1st. ed., p. 127.

[3] 1st. ed., p. 133.

"whatever definition we take, it is not true that all kinds of capital act with equal force in this direction;" but this leaves the fallacy unrectified. His proposition remains that increase either of saved claim to wealth or of, say, machinery, generally tends to increase the demand for labour and so to raise wages. Now, it would be a mere quibble to say that increase of machine plant augments the demand for labour in respect that labour was needed to make the new machinery, and yet only in that sense would the proposition be valid. New machinery, once made, can be employed only when there is demand for what it will produce; and saved money-claim will, similarly, only be put to the employment of new labour when there is supposed to be demand for what it can do, or hope of underselling other labour, which will be thrown idle. To demand we always return. When again Professor and Mrs. Marshall write that "The demand for labour in a district cannot in the long run be increased by any device that does not lead to an increase of the supply of capital in it,"[1] they are plainly right if they simply mean that increased employment of labour means increased consumption of food and tools, and so forth. But it does not at all follow that there must also be an increase of that nominal "saving" of money which, in the exposition of Mr. and Mrs. Marshall, as in that of "orthodox" economists in general, is sure to be understood (whatever they may have meant) from their repetition of the old formula about capital being a result of saving. And the futility of that formula

[1] *Economics of Industry*, p. 16.

in any case is now clear, when we recognise that mere mutual trust as between producers will lead to the creation of fresh capital in the concrete form of plant and stock, which but for such mutual confidence would not have come into existence, the really "saved" food-capital remaining in either case the same.

But if, finally, industrial confidence means the movement of products and the spontaneous creation of actual capital = products, then the saving of "claim to wealth" is no necessary part of the process of wealth-creation even in a competitive community. And as industrial confidence is notoriously commensurate with activity of demand, the creation of wealth can obviously be promoted by the substitution of an ideal of consumption for an ideal of parsimony.

Here, however, it will be well to carry the exposition briefly to its sociological conclusions. These are (a) that as consumption cannot be indefinitely increased in quantity of each product for each individual, the ideal must be in the main one of rising quality —the consumption of things and services which are not mechanically facile of production; and (b) that as such raising of the standard of consumption is impossible among a blindly multiplying population, the limiting of families is indispensable to the proposed transformation.

II. The foregoing reasoning involves the rejection of the doctrine that national wealth is to be measured by the totals either of banked credit or of the values which measure individual claim to wealth. I have said that Lauderdale devoted an unanswerable chapter to the refutation of this notion. He pointed out that on the system of computation which began in the seventeenth century and flourishes still,[1] national wealth is actually estimated in terms of popular hardship, since that increase in values which arises from relative scarcity is included among the individual riches which are totalled. He laid it down on the contrary that

"In proportion as the riches of individuals are increased by an augmentation of the value of any commodity, the wealth of the society is generally diminished ; and in proportion as the mass of individual riches is diminished, by the diminution of the value of any commodity, its opulence is greatly increased."[2]

This proposition has been denounced as a "melancholy paradox" by an able writer[3] in a passage which goes on to praise the "masterly exposition" of Ricardo's chapter on "Value and Riches," in which Lauderdale's doctrine is actually embodied. Ricardo, it is true, goes through the form of refuting Lauderdale on one contention : but he is really affirming the same thing as Lauderdale does ; and if he drew up his own index, we are forced to conclude that he did not realise what Lauderdale was driving at. The index reference to Lauderdale runs : "his theory that the

[1] Compare his citations from Petty, King, Hooke, Pulteney, and Beeke, pp. 39, 40.

[2] Work cited, p. 49. *Cf.* p. 57.

[3] P. J. Stirling, *The Philosophy of Trade*, 1846, p. 10. This writer among other things made important corrections of Ricardo's doctrine of rent.

scarcity and monopoly of a commodity increase wealth,"
which is the exact reverse of Lauderdale's position.
Lauderdale used "riches" to describe individual claim
to wealth, and pointed out that the nominal adding
together of individual riches did not represent real
national wealth at all. Ricardo, of course, admits
that scarcity of commodity would "enrich" the
holders. He writes :—

> "Let water become scarce," says Lord Lauderdale, "and be
> exclusively possessed by an individual, and you will increase his
> riches, because water will then have value; and if wealth be the
> aggregate of individual riches, you will by the same means also
> increase wealth. You undoubtedly will increase the riches of
> this individual, but inasmuch as . . . all men give up a portion
> of their possessions for the sole purpose of supplying themselves
> with water, which they before had for nothing, they are poorer
> . . . and the proprietor of water is benefited precisely by the
> amount of their loss."

Quite so. But inasmuch as the nominal values of
the transferred possessions remain, the " total of individual riches," in Lauderdale's sense, has increased by
the nominal value of the (unconsumed and prospective)
water, though, in the terms of the case, the well-being
of the majority has diminished. And if for a promptly
consumed commodity like water, we substituted a
fixed commodity like land, the case would be still
clearer. The upshot is, as Ricardo puts it, that
"value is not the measure of riches," when by
"riches" you understand, not individual claim to
wealth, which was Lauderdale's definition, but what
Lauderdale called public wealth. He and Ricardo
were at one, the opposed doctrine being that of the

Physiocrats, who, as before noted, counted a rise of prices as an addition to national wealth. And that very doctrine is subsumed in the estimates of national wealth which still pass current, and in the notion that "savings" are part of such wealth. The economic truth is accurately put by Ruskin in the formula that riches are "a power like that of electricity, acting only through inequalities or negations of itself. The force of the guinea you have in your pocket depends wholly on the default of a guinea in your neighbour's pocket."[1] And the final sociological truth is that "savings" in the last resort represent a power to extort the labour of those who have been unable to "save," from having to toil for bare life from their childhood, or being ill-fitted for a life of struggle.

Nor is this all. Not only does the system of saving offer no special security for the continuance of industry, but it constitutes a visibly and peculiarly disastrous means of misdirecting human energy. Few economic hypotheses are more audacious than the orthodox assumption that invested "savings" are sure to be set to employing labour "productively." To begin with, everybody is quite well aware that much of the saved claim to wealth passes to borrowing States, who spend it on implements of slaughter which in a generation grow obsolete even at that; and to the mere buying of foreign land. But it is further notorious that of the annual savings of claim

---

[1] *Unto this Last*, p. 40. Compare Coleridge: "Half the wealth of this country is purely artificial—existing only in and on the credit given to it by the integrity and honesty of the nation." *Table Talk*, March 20th, 1831.

to wealth an immense mass passes away, even on the
bankers' books, in respect of futile undertakings for
the production of certain forms of wealth. Mill,
coming in his fourth book [1] to a question with which
he ought to have grappled in connection with his so-
called Fundamental Propositions, admits that there
goes on a great waste of capital in periods of over-
trading and speculation. Noticing the fact thus late
in the day, he pronounces it "so simple and con-
spicuous that some political economists, especially M.
de Sismondi and Dr. Chalmers, have attended to it
almost to the exclusion of all other" causes of hind-
rance to the downward tendency of profits. But it is
not merely in "periods" of over-trading that this loss
goes on : the financial journalists chronicle an annual
loss of many millions. And this loss takes place because the kind of stimulus given by "saving" to production is so ill-related to the real needs of the community, setting up as it so often does a speculation on
increased demand when actual demand seems to be
provided for. A regimen of consumption would not
incur these disasters of the regimen of parsimony ;
that is to say, it would not mean the gambling of
producers for large hauls on which to subsist by way
of investment.

It is only right to admit that these annual mis-
calculations of capitalists benefit the workers in respect that they really mean processes of consumption.
"What is saved is consumed," as the orthodox formula
has it. And this brings us to one more refutation of
orthodoxy—of the doctrine, that is to say, that "the

---

[1] Ch. iv., *Of the Tendency of Profits to a Minimum.*

destruction of things is not good for trade."[1] Seeing
that the same creed has all along contemplated the
mere consumption (destruction) of saved capital as
constituting the benefit derived by the workers from
capital, we have here a mere dogmatic suicide.
Orthodoxy is reduced once more to the Leibnitzian
position that it is "good for trade" to consume at a
certain rate (else all trade is a perpetuity of disaster),
but not to consume any quicker; and that ordinary
commerce sets the right rate.

"It is not good for trade," we are told, "to have dresses made
of material which wears out quickly. For if people did not
spend their means on buying new dresses, they would spend
them on giving employment to labour in some other way."[2]

Why, what does it matter to "trade" whether I
employ three men in making flimsy clothes or one in
making strong clothes and two in making an orrery?
The orthodox position frequently resolves itself into
denying that wanton destruction, e.g., the smashing of
window-panes, is good for trade.[3] The argument is,
that the money that has to be spent on mending the
windows is withheld from the employment of labour

---

[1] Mr. and Mrs. Marshall, *Economics of Industry*, p. 17.

[2] *Ibid.*

[3] When the main part of this essay was read to the Political
Economy circle of the National Liberal Club, the main defence
offered to the criticism on Mill was that his doctrine, "Demand
for commodities is not demand for labour," really meant that
mere destruction of property did not help to employ labour.
But the impartial reader must see, first, that this is not at all
Mill's drift, and, second, that the doctrine is economically idle.
It is a part of the wages fund theory.

of other kinds. But that does not follow. Where
the spender is one of the "saving" class, the presumption is that he merely fails to "save" the money
in question. Had he saved it, that amount of claim
to wealth might have lain idle in the bank for weeks
or months, or been borrowed by a gambler; or it
might have gone to employ labour in making gun-
powder in Russia, or to employ or over-employ some
labour at home. In the former cases it gave no impulse to production. In the latter case the investment would come to the same thing with the spending
labour in either case was employed, whether to make
new panes not in demand or to put panes into sashes.
The only difference would be that in the process of
investment part of the claim was diverted to the
maintenance of the banking class. Since "what is
saved is consumed," the question comes to this, Which
class is to do any given portion of the consuming?
In a community where the burdens of labour fell upon all, the breaking of window-panes would be a
waste of labour representing a common loss; but in a
community where one section has accumulated a mass
of claim to future services, and is concerned to get for
its transferred claim a perpetual tribute of new claim,
those who have no accumulated claim are employed
or unemployed just as their employers see chances of
accumulating claim by production. And as employment is clearly more abundant when consumption is
abundant, and often dwindles while there is plenty of
"savings" seeking investment, it is clear that no
stimulus to demand in one direction need necessarily
check it in another, and that no drain on savings need

necessarily check profitable production. Of course, in practice it does do so when the savers decide to consume still less ; but the fact that such abstinence checks production is the refutation of the doctrine that saving promotes production. The economic sophist cannot be allowed to employ both arguments alternately. What is clear is that the consumer, whether he saves or spends, is considering merely his own private interest, and not at all that of the community. And why should the economist suddenly demand from the workman an other-regarding scrupulosity which he never suggests to the man who saves? It is idle. A broken pane is a means of putting so much consumption in the way of the glazier. And as the problem for each labour class is just to do its share of consuming the "remuneratory capital" available, the glaziers must needs rejoice when the stress of a riot falls on windows and not on hats.

The spectacle is, indeed, painful from the point of view of an enlightened humanism ; but that standpoint cannot be taken by the advocate of the principle of saving for productive investment. When the motive force of "saved" money capital is not being spent on pure futility, it is as often as not producing bad goods to undersell better. In commerce, under the regimen of parsimony, every producer seeks to produce as much as possible without consuming any more of the products that others are multiplying, much less calling for new products of a higher order which might divert labour from the abundant sorts. The Smithian economists insist that "general" over-production is impossible, meaning really "universal" over-production. J. B. Say and Ricardo established the doctrine that, as goods exchange for goods, all supply *is* demand, and over-production is impossible [1] —a tenacious fallacy, consequent on the inveterate evasion of the plain fact that men want for their goods, not merely some other goods to consume, but further, some credit or abstract *claim to future wealth, goods, or services.* This all want as a surplus or bonus, and this surplus cannot be represented for all in present goods. On Say's theory, there could be no profit save what was immediately realised by extra consumption, and such consumption he deprecated. In Mill's hands, the sophism loses none of its outrageousness. Proceeding complacently, like his predecessors, to refute those who pointed to the glaring evils of gluts, he triumphantly explains that if only *other* things were as freely produced there would be

---

[1] Say, *Traité*, L. I. ch. xv., *Des Debouchés.* Ricardo, *Principles*, ch. xxi. It is noteworthy, however, that Ricardo modified his first emphatic statement. In his first edition (p. 362) he writes : "Productions are always bought by productions or by services ; money is only the medium by which the exchange is effected. Hence the increased production being always accompanied by a correspondingly increased ability to get and consume, there is no possibility of over-production." The passage is thus quoted by Messrs. Mummery and Hobson, whose book is described in our next chapter. But in the second and later editions the second sentence disappears, and the argument simply goes on to the effect that "too much of a *particular* commodity may be produced," but not of *all* commodities, which is an idle truism. J. B. Say also notes that the commodities required to buy others must be "of the right sort," which reduces the general doctrine to a quibble.

no gluts. And this comfort is offered to the thousands of producers who know that *their* products are often in excess of effective demand, in the face of the mathematical certainty that all other products *cannot* be so multiplied. Mill himself, in his worst manner, [1] points out that money is a commodity like another, and that a superfluity of that would mean rising prices, which would negate a glut. He might have added that land (to say nothing of credits) is a commodity not producible in excess of demand. He is arguing that there will be no glut if everything is multiplied, when he knows everything cannot be. And while perpetrating this paralogism, and making the incredible assumption that his opponents were afraid of *universal* over-production, he writes of the "fatal misconception" which has "spread like a veil between them and the more difficult portions of the subject, not suffering one ray of light to penetrate."

In Mill's case the optimistic doctrine is peculiarly preposterous, because, as we have seen, he had before laid it down that the only way in which capital could keep industry always going, was by employing labour at first hand without profit. But if in Mill's case the capitalists had to ignore one chapter in order to derive

---

[1] B. III., ch. xiv. sec. 2. Sismondi (*Etudes sur l'Economie Politique*, 1837, i., 79 ; iii., 314) advanced the very fact of the impossibility of exchanging the same kind of goods *ad infinitum* in a fixed population as a plain refutation of the sophism that all supply is demand. So Stirling (*Philosophy of Trade*, p. 55) pointed out in 1846, that "labour and the products of agriculture cannot be increased in the same ratio or with the same facility as the products of manufacturing industry."

encouragement from another, they had a more single-minded support elsewhere. Ricardo explicitly set forth,[1] (and this proposition he did not recast) that " Mr. Say has most satisfactorily shown that there is no amount of capital which may not be employed in a country, because demand is only limited by production." True, even Ricardo found Mr. Say imperfectly sound in his own faith.

" Is the following," he asks in a footnote, "quite consistent with Mr. Say's principle ?   ' *The more [that] disposable capitals are abundant in proportion to the extent of employment for them, the more will the rate of interest on loans of capital fall*'—(*Traité* ii., 108). If capital to any extent can be employed in a country, how can it be said to be abundant, compared with the extent of employment for it ? "

How indeed ! And how could Ricardo leave the matter with that comment, knowing as he did that lendable "capital" *did* vary in abundance ? By implication, he would have to answer that the undertakers had merely failed to employ capital as they might—a proposition disallowed by his whole habit of economic reasoning. The truth is, that Say's expression was a fresh surrender of his doctrine that supply is demand, for if he repeated the sophism that what was wanted was production of a different sort of commodities, he had no way of explaining why these commodities were not produced when capital was admittedly available—no way, that is, save admitting that consumption-demand is the limit of each kind of production. Nor could Ricardo offer any other

---

[1] As last cited.

explanation. But, committed like the rest to the gospel of saving and investment, he allowed the old doctrine of unlimited saving to stand in the teeth of the current refutations, and the undertakers held by the doctrine that chimed with their main inclinations —that is, if they thought of doctrine at all.

Whether or not they study the economists, the producers of popular goods have chronically exemplified the fatal tendency of the "saving" ideal towards the stage of carrying the industrial head under the industrial arm. Periodically do they find themselves outrunning demand ; and though there does now seem to be a tendency towards rational organisation, it must be hard for the capital-hunter to keep short of fatality while the regimen of parsimony subsists. Over-production is chronic ; and all the while, in the face of that kaleidoscopic principle that he who supplies also demands, the over-producer (master and workman alike) is exhorted to sell as far as possible without buying, to "save" as much as possible of his wages, or the money or credit which he is paid for his goods, so as to cause that to be applied to—further production ! In that case, does not his capital buy plant or labour ? As for the goods produced, why, these must be left to the chances of trade. Thus are still more goods produced without being consumed, and, in self-preservation, inferior goods are produced to undersell the others, till at length nothing will serve but the dismissal of workmen.[1] So that, at any one moment of

---

[1] Doubtless the fall in prices benefits the workers before the collapse comes, just as waste of capital in bad schemes feeds them. Thus it turns out that the miscalculation of

commercial history, there is either over-production, crisis, or strategic check of production ; and all the while multitudes are perforce striving not to consume what they might, so that they may have something to fall back on in sickness or idleness. And all the more surely the idleness comes, and they do fall back on it. And thus life is narrowed and degraded, products made poorer, dwellings more paltry, so that the collective " comfort " of the industrial population is something immeasurably ignoble, like the pullulating of rabbits and mice. A great industrial city of to-day represents a poverty, in some of the main elements of pleasurable life, such as would have appalled a Greek or Roman : the *public wealth* of the greatest city in the industrial era is sordid penury compared with that of a city of antiquity.

From the most enlightened commercial standpoint, which here coincides with the orthodox economic tradition, future development is to be merely a matter of multiplying the conditions of cheap existence. The forethoughtful trader, that is, sees that production of ordinary machine-made commodities is always out-running demand ; and puts his faith only in " new markets " for these same commodities, in Africa or elsewhere. Even Mill, after all his polemic about employing bricklayers, and the impossibility of " general "

the manufacturer, which Smith put on a level with the prodigality of the spendthrift as tending to national impoverishment, is, like that, a cause of popular gain. The spendthrift's purchases, in many cases, go into the second-hand market at greatly reduced prices ; and he and the unlucky manufacturer have thus both promoted "public opulence." The trouble sets in when the manufacturer shuts up his factory.

gluts, comes at long last[1] to this view, making no attempt to bring it into harmony with his optimism. He accepts as "substantially true" the proposition of Wakefield[2] that "production is limited not solely by the quantity of capital and of labour, but also by the extent of the 'field of employment;'" and then we have this commentary :—

"The error which seems to me imputable to Mr. Wakefield is that of supposing his doctrines to be in contradiction to the principles of the best (!) school of preceding political economists, instead of being, as they really are, corollaries from these principles ; *though corollaries which, perhaps, would not always have been admitted by those political economists themselves.*"

Such a vindication of the "preceding" economists needs no discussion. The point is that, just as his "fundamental" prescription for the employment of labour was an indefinite multiplication of work for work's sake, so his independent common-sense conclusion is that we can only jog on by opening up new markets for the most facile products of labour. With all his genuine humane aspiration, he will in no wise see that the line of upward progress can only be through an ideal of increasing and refining consump-

---

[1] B. IV., ch. iv., sec. 2.

[2] Author of *England and America* (1834), and editor of an edition of Smith's *Wealth of Nations*. In the former he exposed (pp. 74-89) somewhat diffusely, not only the prevailing fallacy as to unlimited accumulation of capital, but the glaring contradiction between the doctrine of capital and wages and the actual state of things in America. In his edition of Smith (1835, ii., 387-390) he criticises the doctrine of parsimony, admitting that his views were suggested to him by passages of Chalmers.

tion all round. And what Mill would not see, the
trader naturally will not.

There is one last encouragement to the ideal of
parsimony which should be noticed, by way of con-
stating all the forces of the situation. In one way, or
at one point, the saving system can be seen directly
to add to national wealth—I say national wealth, ad-
visedly. Mill notes [1] that in "old countries" the
tendency to fall in profits "is stopped at the point
which sends capital abroad." That is the beginning
of the really public advantage. "Money" lent abroad
must needs go in the form of home products, in making which the workers get permits to consume ; and
for these products there comes back, in a certain number of cases, an annual tribute of interest in the shape
of foreign products, which are thus cheapened to us
in general. Of course foreign investments in English
stocks and industries draw a tribute from us *per
contra*, but the Board of Trade returns thus far show
a surplus of imports over exports (whereat the blun-
derers lament); and while the experts can give the
true interpretation of this, the "saving" class are not
likely to be discountenanced in their ideal by the consideration that the gain comes of a perpetual lien on
the labour of alien poor. Thus is the economic fallacy
buttressed. [2]

---

[1] B. IV., ch. v., sec. 1.

[2] The argument is so used by Dr. Walcker (*Lehrbuch*, p. 37).
He notes that "a rich Englishman may buy Russian railway
preferences, and thereby promote the well-being of the English
people with cheaper Russian corn." But he does not stay to
ask what is the effect on the well-being of the Russian people.
In the terms of the case, it must be to make corn dearer to them.

CHAPTER VIII.

"THE PHYSIOLOGY OF INDUSTRY"—A CONFIRMATORY ARGUMENT.

SINCE this essay was first written, there has appeared a treatise which so ably and effectively sets forth the same doctrine, that only the difference in my method of approach makes the publication of mine still advisable. It is *The Physiology of Industry*, by Messrs. A. F. Mummery and J. A. Hobson.[1] "An Exposure of Certain Fallacies in Existing Theories of Economics" is the sub-title; and the fallacies exposed are in particular those dealt with in the foregoing chapters. But Messrs. Mummery and Hobson have made their analysis, as it were, from the other end, taking the received doctrine and comparing it with the actual processes of industry, both abstractly and concretely, analysing rather these processes than the teaching which misrepresents them, and finally grounding their refutation on their exposition of the real processes of the industrial system in the concrete. It is the more satisfactory to me, and it will perhaps be the more noteworthy to the reader, that from the different lines of approach the conclusion as to the Fallacy of Saving is arrived at with equal emphasis in both cases.

---

[1] London : John Murray. 1889.

Messrs. Mummery and Hobson, without dwelling on
the history of the doctrine of parsimony, attack it in
John Mill's statement as I have done, but they give
us the profit of a confirmatory argument by working
consistently on those definitions of capital and saving
which were set forth, but not consistently adhered to,
by the older economists. They confute Mill and the
later writers as Lauderdale confuted Smith. I cannot think that the use of this definition in a general
discussion is the best way of enlightening the ingenuous student; at all events, I have sought to impress
on him that the old definitions of capital and saving
do not quadrate with the facts and the speech of
everyday affairs. But for the purpose of confutation,
Messrs. Mummery and Hobson's method is irresistible.

Capital they define,[1] after a survey of the difficulties and exigencies of the case, as "(1) Raw
material and goods in their various stages of development, including shop-goods; (2) plant and all
machinery;" and saving they define[2] as "the difference between what is produced and what is consumed. The correct formula is as follows: production
—consumption = savings." On these definitions the
old doctrine can be tested with the utmost logical
rigour. As the authors observe,[3] capital "has been
described as 'the result of saving' by those who have
not yet explained what saving means, and who afterwards appear to include in savings, the food which is
not saved but consumed by labourers." Their own
definition precludes confusion by clearly excluding

---

[1] Page 34.   [2] Page 36.   [3] Page 31.

the process of what commonly passes for saving, *i.e.*, the "putting-by" of money or credits. And on this basis it becomes instantly apparent that, as they put it, "A belief in the infinite possibility of saving implies a belief in the infinite increase of consumption,"[1] precisely what the exhortation to saving aims at limiting. Messrs. Mummery and Hobson here seize and expose the fallacy as I have sought to do in the opening examination of Smith ; noting in turn that Mill's doctrine of saving stultifies itself, inasmuch as

"The new labourers have already got a stock of necessaries provided for them in the new wages fund, constantly maintained by a continuance of the former abstinence of the capitalists. The wealth, then, which the new labourers produce must either go to provide luxuries for themselves or for the old class of labourers, or it must provide luxuries for the capitalists, who will thus be obliged to revoke their vow of abstinence. To one or two, or all of these uses, it must be put, and in any case it will be unproductively consumed in the shape of luxuries."[2]

In fine, we may put it that Mill's doctrine in practice would work out the artificial and gratuitous multiplication of the poorest sort of labourers,[3] which we know was certainly not his social ideal. And as to Mill's successors, Messrs. Mummery and Hobson, too, note[4] how, "strange to say, those who have most distinctly repudiated the wage fund theory have retained the theory of the possibility of infinite saving, which depended on it." On the general survey of the broad relation of production to consumption, they themselves sum up[5] that "if increased

[1] Page 37. [2] Page 45. [3] Page 49. [4] Page 46. [5] Page 51.

thrift or caution induces people to save more in the present, they must consent to consume more in the future." That is, of course, as regards "the production and consumption of the entire community;"[1] for, of course, as between individuals, the balancing consumption can be and is done by others than the savers in so far as it is finally done at all.

Now comes the independent analysis of "the physiology of production," in which it appears that " to the maker and the trader, goods, raw material, plant, etc., are valued exclusively for the more or less of *purchasing power* which they afford to their owners," and that, "from the point of view of the individual tradesman, all acts of sale and purchase are primarily exchanges of forms of this purchasing power." Thus, the price the baker gets for his bread keeps his capital intact when the bread is sold, the capital being merely in a constant alternation of forms; and only the act of consumption extinguishes a portion of purchasing power and annihilates "a portion of the total stock of wealth of the community."[2] (To be more strictly accurate, it should be put that the baker is always slightly increasing his purchasing power or capital in respect of his profit on sales, and that he may or may not continuously extinguish the increase by his private consumption.) Two propositions are in this way established :—

"Firstly, that an exercise of demand (for commodities) *cannot diminish capital;* secondly, that an exercise of demand,

---

[1] Page 53.   [2] Pages 60, 61.

though it consumes a portion of previously existent wealth and annihilates a portion of purchasing power, causes the production of an equivalent amount of new forms of wealth and purchasing power"—

that is, in respect that the act of purchase passes back as a wave of impetus along the whole producing series to the first member of it, and causes fresh production. I have said that Messrs. Mummery and Hobson consistently apply the definition of capital as a set of concretes; but it is not quite clear that they do so at this point. We are here in face of a constant transmutation of a concrete into an abstract, and *vice versa*; and the act of consuming a portion of concrete stock (till then = capital) is balanced by setting in motion an abstract force, which is the only representative of the given amount of capital till the new stock is made. Is not capital then here something else as well as what it was defined to be? True, the authors have pointed out [1] that when half the machines in a factory are idle, or all are used only at half-time or half-pressure, "the real capital consists in half the machines, the other half being surplus or nominal capital;" and as they show (as did Lauderdale), that there may easily be concrete fixed capital of certain sorts in excess of the existing needs of the whole community, it would follow that when "purchasing power" in the form of saved credit is in excess of the industrial needs of the time (which we have seen is constantly the case), such excess is only nominal and not real capital. But that

---

[1] Page 35.

does not alter the fact that just as the unused
machines still figure as capital in the owner's estimate, so the superfluous saved money-credit figures
as capital. And though, as we have decided, the
superfluous saved money-credit would immensely
raise prices if it were all at once sought to be realised
in any or all of the existing forms of concrete wealth,
thus demonstrating its illusoriness, yet any one portion of it still subsists as purchasing power, and it is
impossible to say what portions of it are "real"
capital and what are not. And this brings us back to
the question of what is really the best definition of
capital. The question is not, it has been well said,
What *is* capital, but What is capital to be? Messrs.
Mummery and Hobson write :—

"If we are unable to say whether a particular piece of wealth
which exists is or is not at the present time capital, it is absurd
to maintain that our term capital can be a useful part of our
economic nomenclature."[1]

But is not the philosophic form of statement just
this, that a particular piece of wealth, or, in Mr.
Macleod's phrase, any *economic quantity*, is or is
not capital according as it stands or does not stand in
the "capital" or "principal" relation to an industrial
or commercial process? Defined in this way, capital
is as clearly specified as any concept whatever, and
we are at once delivered from all concrete confusion,
to the great gain of economic logic. The word will
cover, at need, alike concretes and abstracts, goods
and plant and credit and claim. And the only stipu-

---

[1] Page 31.

lation necessary to be made all round is that all
writers shall make an end of the pretence of adding
up "the capital of the country," and of the use of
language about "additions to the total capital of the
country,"—verbal processes which were always practically absurd, and are now specifically so. Defined
as above—and this, I maintain, is the only philosophic definition—general or national capital is an
infinity ; and if we are to total anything included in
it, it must be specifically, as plant, and stock, and
machine-power, and water-power, and acreage, and
productivity, and working hands. To add up credit
or claim is futile. And Messrs. Mummery and
Hobson, it seems to me, are finally committed to this
reasoning and this definition. They explicitly state[1]
that "since the community, as a whole, can never consume more 'subsistence, convenience, and amusements'
than it has actually produced, it is obvious that the
community [= the whole industrial public, not the
nation as a receiver and spender through its political
executive] can never live beyond its income." But
the same line of analysis works out the conclusion
that the community as a whole can never live beyond
its capital, since as we have seen every act of effective
demand, involving a recognised claim, goes to set up
fresh production, and there is no necessary limit to
credit. And this truth, as it happens, was formulated
two hundred years ago, by one Dr. Bifield, cited by
Lauderdale. A person, says Bifield, can waste his
stock, "because his waste is finite : but the stock of
a nation is infinite, and can never be consumed ; for

---

[1] Page 78.

what is infinite can neither receive addition by parsimony, nor suffer diminution by prodigality." [1]   This
was written in 1690.   The mills of economics have
ground exceeding slow.

So much for theory.   As to practice, Messrs.
Mummery and Hobson sum up dead against the
doctrine of parsimony.   Treating Mill's worst formula
with the greatest consideration, they observe [2] that he
"rightly contended that the demand for shop goods
was not the demand for the labour which had previously produced them" (a pleasing truism which, I
suppose, expresses the elusive truth recognised in the
doctrine by Mr. Leslie Stephen); and they point out
that "it by no means follows that present demand for
shop goods is not the source of present demand for
labour," but that, on the contrary, "the use of natural
agents, capital, and labour, produces commodities, and
demand for these commodities is demand for the
[further] use of the requisites of production." [3]   And
now comes the sociological conclusion [4] :—

"The identification of depression in trade with insufficient
consumption or excessive thrift is, we venture to assert, un-
assailable. . . .   This conclusion is of critical importance to the
community : it means neither more nor less than that the community *could at once and permanently enjoy a larger income.*   It
means that the East End problem, with its concomitants of vice
and misery, is traced to its economic cause, and that this
economic cause is the most respectable and highly extolled
virtue of thrift."   .

---

[1] *A Discourse of Trade*, by H. Bifield, M.D., printed 1690,
cited by Lauderdale, p. 222, *note*.

[2] Page 92.   [3] Page 95.   [4] Page 99.

Substantially as I am in agreement with this conclusion in its economics, I will take leave to suggest certain qualifications which are necessary to make it strictly accurate. First of all, it is necessary to keep in view that the under-consumption which is specified as the cause of trade depression must not be understood as a regrettable under-consumption of the things of which there is a glut. This brings us to the grain of truth involved (unconsciously to them) in the old optimists' maxim, that the cure for a glut was extended production of the things of which there is not a glut. Not that the cure would or could operate as they supposed. The one way, on their principles, to cure a glut of boots and hats would be to consume these wastefully in exchange against other things, since mere increase of population, though thus encouraged by implication, could only after an interval of time dispose of a present overplus. And the increase of population, on the old lines of parsimony and production, could mean ultimately nothing but new and greater periodic gluts. The real cure, as regards the labour-market, would be by way of *extension of demand to objects not readily produced in excess;* such as superior hand-made goods and products of *art* of all kinds. Here a glut is impossible, provided only that the standard of taste goes on rising with the many as it has done with the few. Art is longer than life, and there lies the true philosopher's stone of perpetual industry—the reaching towards an end forever unattained. It is not quantity but *kind* of consumption, the setting up a continuous demand which shall withdraw labour from the fatally

II

easy fruitions of the mechanical manufacture of common necessaries, that will prevent chronic depression
of trade. And such ever-rising standard of demand,
it is obvious, is impossible without such a restraint of
the rate of increase of population as shall give scope
for the play of the higher and subtler needs without
fatal encroachment on the part of the simpler and
lower. These things Messrs. Mummery and Hobson
should have stated as sociologists, since it is their
aim and their merit to carry their economics into
sociology.

Secondly, they overstate the sociological, and therefore the economic, case for consumption when they
teach that simple increase of consumption may solve
the "East End problem." For one thing, large families
must always mean relative poverty under a wage-
earning system, and, if numerous, comparative poverty,
up to the revulsion point, in a socialistic system. For
another thing, it must not be forgotten (some im-
patient readers, it may be, have long ere this accused
us of forgetting) that old people cannot work to their
last day for their own support, and that under a
regimen of increased and increasing consumption,
while healthy wage-earners (barring over-population)
will certainly have a better income, there will be ne-
cessitated a new social machinery for supporting the
aged. At present the aged poor (such as can become
aged) go to the workhouse, or subsist painfully on
small club allowances, while the less poor subsist on
the fruits of their savings, that is, on the interest of
their accumulated money-claim on the services of
others. Now, it is idle to suppose that while the

workhouse remains the only common provision for old age, those capable of saving will abstain from doing so. The instinct of self-preservation will continue to assert itself; and either the battle of saving will be intensified as more and more persons accumulate claim, or there will ensue such demoralisation of the wage-earning proletariat as took place in the proletariat of ancient Rome, unless a rational system of corporate action be developed. One or other of these three courses our civilisation must take; because even the all-essential restraint of population cannot alone secure that all who work shall have a moiety of the comfort now enjoyed by those who do not work at all, though it would greatly modify the atrocity of the present scramble for employment and the misery of the lower strata. Even a controlled population acting on the principle of parsimony will be one in which machinery will rapidly overtake the total demand for necessaries, as it has already overtaken again and again the effective demand, so that even in such a society there would be, barring organisation, chronic industrial crises. A rising demand for the higher products is as essential as control of procreation. Moreover, the struggle of saving would grow more and more internecine in a community in which restraint of population minimised the helpless mass, and he who would live on his investments must save more and more to outsave his competitors. In the words of Messrs. Mummery and Hobson,[1] "Each is competing against the other; each is seeking to do

___

[1] Page 112.

himself the largest portion of the useful saving." But
when there is any constant quantity of economically
superfluous saving, it is clear, cancelment is in the
main (allowing for variations of luck) a process affecting all sums of savings proportionately, and he who
has the largest total will always have the largest
amount of effective claim. Thus the struggle must
go from bad to worse, with no relief but that chronically and partially supplied by the annihilation of
masses of money-credit in desperate enterprises.

Expanding consumption, then, is not enough: restraint of population must go with it. And it is clear
that expanding consumption, with or without restraint
of population, involving, as it must, the surrender of
the present means of self-preservation for the more or
less successful in old age, will never be adopted as the
general ideal until some common provision for old age
is set on foot.

In these conclusions, I think, Messrs. Mummery
and Hobson must acquiesce. It is clearly not enough
to say, as they do in one place,[1] that " if the community
wishes to increase its capital, it must consent to increase its consumption," for there is always going on
an increase in mass of consumption, and consequently
in capital in their sense, by force of the mere increase
of population. To the wider conclusion they are led
by their demonstration of

" the fundamental fallacy which underlies the economists'
view of saving, the assumption that the interests of the community must always be identical with the interests of its several
members. The statement of Adam Smith, ' what is prudence

---

[1] Page 112.

in the conduct of a private family can scarce be folly in that of a great nation,' has been taken too generally for a gospel truth. This view, that a community means nothing more than the addition of a number of individual units, and that the interests of society can be ascertained by adding together the interests of individual members, has led to as grave errors in economics as in other branches of sociology." [1]

These general conclusions, I submit, have now been proved, and no less the particular.

For the rest, Messrs. Mummery and Hobson supply a close and cogent analysis of "Over-Production and Economic Checks," which will be found to confirm my own more summary statements on that head. Following out the principle of their first chapter, that the economics of consumption cannot without fallacy be separated from that of production, and that consumption is really only the closing act of production, [2] they have really justified their title of *The Physiology of Industry*, which would hardly have been done by

---

[1] Page 106, citing Smith, B. IV., ch. ii., sec 1. It should be noted that Smith, who generally saw the sound as well as the unsound view of a case sooner or later, though he so often failed to make the proper cancelment, himself remarked in another passage that "the merchants knew perfectly well in what manner to enrich themselves. It was their business to know it. But to know in what manner it enriched the country was no part of their business" (B. IV., ch. i., McCulloch's ed., p. 189); and, still more explicitly, that "the interest of the dealers in any particular branch of trade or manufactures is always in some respect different from, and even opposite to, that of the public " (B. I., ch. xi., *end*).

[2] A view wrought out also by Mr. R. S. Moffat in his *Economy of Consumption*, with much convincing illustration and great expository power.

Mr. Stirling had he called his work, as he at first intended, *The Physiology* instead of *The Philosophy of Trade*. They complete the argument, finally, by a refutative chapter on " Scarcity of Gold as an Economic Factor," to which those readers may turn who feel that the arguments of the currency school call for detailed answer. I apprehend, however, that those who acquiesce in the present argument thus far will not demur to my leaving those arguments on one side.

PART II.—THE PRACTICAL ISSUE.

I.

ALREADY, perhaps, the reader, in accepting the argument, has recoiled in despair from the vast vista of social reconstruction which it opens up as the only alternative to a long decline towards darkness. He may be moved to cry out with Mr. Lang, and with perhaps the better justification as having really tried to understand the case, that "the social problem is insoluble," and that after a few centuries we shall just "worry back to barbarism." There is a certain sombre fascination in this species of pessimism that especially captures the belletrist mind, even that mind which, in resentment of other austere philosophies, formulates for itself in the name of mythological science the doctrine of a divine "Father who is not far from any one of us,"[1] and is solaced under the pressure of the insoluble social problem by the spectacle of the "beautiful Church of England." But if the belletrist, who at least realises that there is a social problem, is thus impressed by it, we must confess that it will be hard to bring home to his public the falsity of the current economic gospel of saving.

All the forces of egoism and optimism are on its side. As a matter of fact—and this is the real crux

[1] Mr. Lang : *Myth, Ritual, and Religion*, i. 340.

of the case, remaining after all the economic fallacies are
exposed—the average middle-class man has at present
no way open to him *but* saving to provide for his old
age ; that is, the minority must "save" in order to
live one day on the labour of the majority. If the
saver buys an annuity, his money seeks investment
all the same. How make the middle-class multitude
ever realise that this proceeding of theirs is a saving
only of abstract purchasing power : how make them
see, even with the fall of interest before their eyes,
that the more people save, the nearer nullification will
be their mutual claims ; that instead of being a means
by which all can add to the common well-being and
their own, it is only a process by which a saving minority can command the services of a non-saving
majority ? These, we have seen, are the facts. The
increasing "savings" of the working-classes, we repeat
once more, represent no saved or made property of any
kind, but an abstract *claim to wealth*, which to seek at
once to realise would be to prove the unreality of the
wealth by immensely raising prices. It is practically
a claim on services in general, and these services are
only realisable in so far as alongside of the savers
there remains a multitude which saves nothing or
little. Let that multitude save also, and cancelment
of claim begins to take place all round. But just as
saving extends, cancelment of claim *is* proportionally
going on, the result being that the more A saves the
more B must save to get the better of him.

Meantime, the cure prescribed for the workers is
that they shall not only be chary of consuming the
goods which they live by producing, but equally ab-

stain from consuming high-class goods, the production
of which would call for labour of a higher class—
labour which could not be superseded by machinery.
And their saved money is consequently to be invested
in the production of only the kinds of goods or services which, so far as parsimony prevails, must of
necessity be forthcoming, and are for the most part
only too easily multiplied. Thus their very savings do
but go to facilitate the crises which throw them idle.
The more they cause "capital" to abound, too, the
more nearly impossible it becomes for them to be their
own capitalists for productive purposes, since the savings of the upper classes go the more to form overwhelming joint-stock concerns that blight smaller
undertakings. Thus, on the one hand, we have the
increasing class of idle rich, living on investments, and
well-to-do jobbers, living by spurious commerce; and,
on the other hand, the increasing class of toiling poor,
who on all hands are taught to aim at investments
likewise, but only here and there to limit their rate of
increase and raise their standards of comfort, though
only by these last courses can they, under any con-
ceivable regimen, countervail the constant extension
of labour-saving machinery, and make new labour independent of the capital of the idlers. We are in such
an *impasse* that even if the National Debt were rapidly
paid off by way of removing a burden from industry,
the result must needs be the throwing idle of many
thousands, through the stinting of the consumption of
fundholders left without investments, unless one of
two courses were pursued. Either (*a*) the principle of
parsimony must be generally abandoned, and the

majority must demand high-class goods or services which should be more or less providable by those who formerly provided nominally high-class goods or services for the fundholders; or (*b*) the State or the municipalities must institute important public works (such as civic reconstruction, with good working-class houses, or comprehensive sewage-schemes), which should extensively employ and train inexpert labour. Indeed, it is clear that the contingency could not be met save by the action of both these general factors: the workers must consume if production is to be kept up. And, finally, restraint of propagation is an indispensable condition of the maintenance of the improved state of affairs.

Now, is there any prospect at present, in the face of the faith in parsimony, that either, on the one hand, the State or the municipalities will institute the necessary constructive works (which would of course have to be based on an extended taxation of rent and incomes), or that, on the other hand, the general public will recast its standards of life and insist on consuming and therefore producing more good things? Is there, again, any prospect that the State or the municipalities will institute a system of provision for old age and sickness, not by a scheme of insurance fallaciously resting on blind investment, but on a system of calculated production of the things people need? And, finally, is there any prospect that the people in general will effect that control of their rate of increase without which both of the other rearrangements would be futile?

As our sociology stands, the prospects are certainly

not bright. Are they then blank? If so, why, then we have been contemplating no mere corrigible fallacy of the reason, but a radical fallacy or flaw in human things—in life itself. And who outside the school of Mr. Lang can accept such a conclusion?

It is certainly a damping reflection that most of the economists who have been cited as seeing through the Fallacy of Saving have negatively or positively failed in their prescriptions for society. Lauderdale, in arguing down the sinking fund principle, had the air of vindicating the National Debt; Sismondi attacked machinery; Mr. Ruskin has done that and rather worse things; Malthus confessedly approved the institution of an idle rich class, and lost weight also by his defence of the Corn Laws, though in that his error was not absolute, seeing that he recognised the new trouble of rapidly multiplied population, to which the Free Traders shut their eyes. Chalmers, again, made a preposterous proposal for the special support of aristocrats; and nearly all these economists in a way seemed to endorse the old notion that labour *necessarily* depends on the expenditure of the idle rich—a doctrine which Mr. Ruskin has on moral grounds gratuitously attacked as being that of the prevailing economists (who, as we have seen, did not hold it), and which was after all only a blundering version of the true doctrine of spending enforced by Mr. Ruskin himself. Later than Malthus and Chalmers, Mr. Moffat, who, like them, has assailed the Fallacy of Saving, has decided to credit the landlords with a moral right to economic rent as the just reward of their activities of superintendence. Nay, even Messrs.

Mummery and Hobson give one a shock of alarm by
offering as an ostensible encouragement to an Eight
Hours Law, what amounts to a *reductio ad absurdum*
of that scheme. This, I think, they must admit; as
I trust they will admit the other sociological considerations urged above in connection with their
conclusions. Their treatment of the Eight Hours
question brought upon them the keen thrust of Mr.
Bradlaugh; and I doubt not they will mend the crack
in their armour. Any way, however, there are
apparently heavy odds against my concluding with a
sound practical solution where so many have either
failed or stopped short. I can but try.

II.

An accomplished economist of the individualist school,
hearing the gist of the foregoing argument read,
gave it as his opinion that the destructive criticism
was unanswerable, but that the constructive sug-
gestions made in the last few pages were unsound. It
was, I doubt not, the suggestion of State action that
was in view in this objection, for my critic agreed
with me as to the absolute necessity of restraint of
population under any regimen. And I am bound to
admit that while this necessity is not generally recognised, State action in the way of providing employment must needs aggravate the industrial trouble by
giving a special stimulus to population. Nay more,
I admit that there are difficulties in the way of resort-
ing to any fresh form of State employment while the
State has not the power of interfering in some way

with over-breeding, even if the necessity of restraint be brought home to the majority by voluntary propaganda such as is going on at present. A certain minority would for a time be reckless, and would add unfairly to the pressure on the community's labour-employing machinery, while profiting by the conscientiousness of others.

The practical answer to this argument is twofold. To begin with, as I have sought to show elsewhere,[1] it is morally incumbent on the community to make an end of the social injustice that is worked by maintaining a National Debt, the interest on which means the support of the idle and comfortable classes by the poor and laborious. All interest on investments, of course, as we have seen in the foregoing analysis, means the same thing in the end; but in the case of the National Debt the community is corporately or politically responsible, and has it in its power by direct and simple action—by the simple process of repayment—to put a stop sooner or later to this particular form of social parasitism. Now, if this moral perception be acted upon, as I think it must be, and the Debt be paid off out of special taxation as rapidly as possible, an acute industrial trouble would arise, unless specially guarded against, in respect of the intensified operation of the saving motive among the investors whose principal was paid down to them. In conformity with the conventional ideal which we have been contemplating—or, let us say, on the spur of the instinct of self-preservation—they will greatly restrict their consumption until they can find new

---
[1] *Modern Humanists*, Epilogue.

investments; and, as we have seen, this must needs
be a very difficult matter. The immediate result,
then, will be a serious industrial depression, since
falling-off in demand for commodities means falling-
off in demand for labour.

It has been objected to my previous exposition[1] that
when the principal of the Debt is paid off, the taxation
thereby remitted, on the score of abolished interest-
payments, will suffice to provide for the extra consumption necessary. But this objection overlooks
three essential points : (1) that in the terms of the
case there had been *extra* taxation to provide for
the payment of the principal, and that this taxation
would, by parity of reasoning, act as a restrictive of
consumption; (2) that the restriction would be
immediate, while the remission of taxation would
only be prospective; and (3) that while the ideal of
saving subsists, there is no security whatever that
remission of taxation will bring about increased or
raised consumption on the part of individuals. My
proposition, then, holds good, that, given a rapid repayment of the National Debt, in the absence of a
general reform in the matter of consumption, which
cannot reasonably be expected to take place quickly,
nothing can avert ruinous industrial depression save
the creation of a special demand for labour by the
corporate action of the community. I can understand
that a determined Individualist will face any amount
of industrial calamity rather than sanction such a
resort to the principle of State Socialism; but I am
bound to declare that, if the circumstances be admitted

---

[1] Epilogue cited.

to be as I say, such determined Individualism amounts to a fanaticism of a very deplorable kind. At best, the Individualist in such a case is purchasing what he regards as safety in the future at the cost of frightful misery in the present. That is to say, he does this if he assents to the demand that the National Debt shall be paid off as rapidly as possible. He has the alternative of leaving the National Debt as it is. In that case, he seems to me to identify his cause with an immense social injustice. Democratic Individualists, I submit, cannot take up such a position.

On the other hand, if those who desire to abolish the injustice do not accept, along with the principle of State employment of labour, that of restriction of population, I can see nothing but new evil ahead. If they *will* accept the principle of restraint, I can conceive matters going substantially well, even without the legal enforcement of restraint, a thing difficult to arrange under any regimen, and plainly impossible in the present state of sociological thought. In view of the continuous fall in the birth-rate, along with an increase in the number of marriages (a clear result of the spread of Neo-Malthusian doctrine), I can conceive that public opinion and voluntary propaganda may ere long so far rationalise the general action that the recklessness of the few will not in itself be ruinous, and will serve to force on the discussion of the principle of legal interference. The more slowly that principle is adopted, the less risk is there of its being crudely or arbitrarily reduced to practice. But if the majority continue to set their faces, as at present, against the very notion of restraint, or tolerate only

ascetic kinds of restraint which it would be idle to
prescribe for general adoption, even if they were
scientifically sound (which they are not), then there
is no escape from an extension of the old trouble.
Nothing short of prudence in procreation can ultimately save the proletariat from chronic hardship.

And one can but hope that the increasing plainness
of the dilemma will ere long bring about the enlightenment of the Liberal politicians who are as yet given
over to helpless empiricism. Already there are signs
that the enlightenment is in process. One Liberal
leader [1] avows an uneasy wish that his party paid
more heed to the population problem. But the chances
are at present that this fundamental sociological principle will be forced on national attention in connection
with a new form of political agitation, which bids
fair to absorb within itself several others. I mean
the demand for Old Age Pensions.

III.

The rapid extension of the vogue of this proposal
within the past year or two is one of the few satisfactory symptoms in industrial politics, from the
scientific point of view. For a time it seemed as if
the demand for an Eight Hours Law was going to
absorb all the self-regarding political energy of the
masses; and the prospect looked sufficiently dark,
because the very failure which must so speedily discredit such a measure as that would go to discredit

---

[1] Mr. John Morley, in a speech to the Eighty Club in 1889.

democratic schemes in general, and a period of inanition would follow that of miscalculation. But the Old Age Pension scheme has the advantage of appealing to the mass of the workers, while being in no way opposed to sound economic principle. The Eight Hours Law would be an economic absurdity worthy of the Middle Ages; a workers' pension scheme—as distinguished, that is, from a system of national insurance—is economically sound. And already, in one form or another, it has been declared for by politicians of different parties; on one side, for instance, by Mr. Chamberlain; on the other side, and on sounder lines, by Dr. W. A. Hunter, whose sagacious advocacy is likely to count for much. But none of its advocates has yet pointed out the weighty economic advantages it may involve; on the contrary, several of its supporters are so far from seeing these that they regard them as imaginary drawbacks, against fear of which the public must be reassured. Mr. Sidney Webb and Mr. Charles Booth, for instance, expressly argue [1] that there is no danger of a pension scheme discouraging thrift; the implication being that, with pensions, the workers will save more and not less—that is to say, will not solidify industry by consuming more and better products. But it will be the principal service a pension system can render, to encourage the workers to consume and not paralyse production by restricting their demand. Evidently we must still justify the pension scheme on economic grounds; and such justification is the more necessary because there

[1] Mr. Webb in the *Contemporary Review*, July, 1890, pp. 103-4; Mr. Booth in a paper which I have not seen.

I

are still some publicists who oppose the pension principle all round.

Of these the most prominent is Mr. C. S. Loch,
Secretary of the London Charity Organisation Society.
Mr. Loch, who has given much professional study to
the phenomena of pauperism, is convinced that it is
largely "created" by loose methods of poor-relief, and
argues [1] that a national pension system would tend to
manufacture it. In so far as the risk is alleged to
arise in terms of the difficulty of escaping malinger-
ing, even among persons over sixty, the point need
not be disputed. Mr. Loch's conclusion is that

"To establish an annuity system, *and not to prohibit out-door
relief to the able-bodied*, or perhaps to all but those who require
medical out-relief, would be to foster a hybrid pauperism, in
part maintained by the rates, in part by imperial and local
taxes." [2]

So be it—barring only the point as to what essentially constitutes pauperism. Let it be provided
that under an adequate pension system out-door relief to the able-bodied shall cease. But Mr. Loch's
theory of pauperism calls for further examination.
Looking at the problem from the standpoint of em-
pirical ethics, he sees in it mainly an outcome of
individual fault; and, what is more, he supposes that
the faults in question, as society is now organised,
constitute a source of unrelieved individual burden to
all who pay the taxes which relieve paupers. But

[1] *Old Age Pensions and Pauperism* (Sonnenschein & Co. 1892),
passim.

[2] Page 41.

that this is not so will be already clear to many who have followed the foregoing economic analysis.

Mr. Loch cites [1] as typically or generally valid an enquiry which discriminates city pauperism as follows :—

" Pauperism caused by old age or infirmity, without any discredit, explained nearly *one-eighth* of the pauperism of the township ; pauperism by disease (not brought on by misconduct) or accidental injuries, involving inability to work, accounted for *one-seventh;* drunkenness explained 51·24 per cent."

Now, it of course never occurs to Mr. Loch that this latter section of pauperism represents anything but an infliction of loss on well-to-do ratepayers generally. He would take that view, presumably, of pauperism attributed to mere improvidence, apart from drunkenness : much more would he take it of drunkenness. And yet it is easy to show that, inasmuch as we have seen the spenders tend to keep industry going while the savers tend to paralyse it by checking consumption and market demand, the victims of improvidence have really sacrificed themselves (un - knowingly, of course) to the advantage of the provident. Had the whole population been alike bent on saving, the total saved would positively have been much less, inasmuch as (other tendencies remaining the same) industrial paralysis would have been reached sooner or oftener, profits would be less, interest much lower, and earnings smaller and more precarious. This, as the reader of the foregoing chapters has seen, is no idle paradox, but the strictest

[1] Page 30.

economic truth.   It follows, then, that since the
spendthrifts facilitate the accumulations of the
savers, the pauper class, in so far as its members
have been industrious but "unthrifty" workers, has
all along been contributing to the general prosperity
as far as it could, while the more fortunate savers
have as such been doing the reverse.   The savers, in
short, have as such been living on the spenders.   Of
course they also have been to some extent spending;
and they may also have been industriously producing;
but in the nature of the case they got their accumulation of purchasing power *from those who parted
with it*, and their accumulations subsist only in so far
as the majority has been willing to go on spending.
To go back to Mr. Ruskin's words, their savings are
valid in virtue of the defect of saving in others.

Apply this to the case of the pauper class, and it
will be seen that even the drunkards have been putting purchasing power in the hands of others.   Of
the "saved" capital or money-credit owned among
the upper classes, enormous sums have come from the
drink trade.   I suppose that even among those who
hold devoutly to the doctrine of saving there will be
hesitation in applauding the brewers and distillers
and publicans for their services in amassing capital.
But in the light of economic analysis it becomes a
peculiarly preposterous hypocrisy to speak of the top-
ing pauper as typically a burden on society while the
brewer and publican are treated as bearers of the
burden.

It will not be supposed, of course, that I deny
the cumulative infelicity of expenditure on drink.

Clearly it not only yields the most transient satisfactions at best, but on the other hand actively negates well-being to the extent of three-fourths of the consumption. But the student has now realised that if all intoxicants were totally abstained from, industrial hardship could only be averted by the setting-up of fresh consumption, which would constitute demand for the labour thrown idle. And the temperance party must be reminded that it does not at all follow that the grain unconsumed by brewers and distillers would continue to be produced, and so lower food prices. That only is produced for which there is market demand. Of course the reformed topers would consume more bread, but that would be all.

We are now in a position to pass judgment on Mr. Loch's conception of pauperism, as bearing on his opposition to a pension system. He is wrong even in his implicit notion that improvidence annihilates purchasing power and lessens the total command of society over wealth and services. He is therefore doubly wrong in his proposition[1] that under a national pension system the present " pauper pensioner would become a pensioner-pauper," and that " pauper he would remain under both guises." That is to say, Mr. Loch is wrong in implying as he unavoidably does that the man who works while he can, and then draws from the public treasury, has deserved ill of society. It cannot be too emphatically declared that the true " paupers " are those who, having done no work whatever, subsist on the interest of savings made by others. We have seen, indeed, that all

[1] Page 27.

subsistence on interest means in practice subsistence
on others' industry; but inasmuch as investment at
interest is the principal means of providing for old
age, those who thus secure themselves are only getting what, broadly speaking, they are entitled to—
setting aside, that is, the question of just share.
When, however, we deal with those who have in-
herited money-capital, and, themselves able-bodied,
live idly on its interest, the same defence does not
hold. They consume services and render none; and
if any are to be socially and economically disparaged,
it is they. I have no wish, indeed, to set up a dis-
paragement which would in its turn operate unjustly,
inasmuch as the idle livers on investments are
actually doing the economic best open to them, in
many cases, when they spend without accumulating
further. But if we are to be considerate to these,
let us be just to those workers who do unquestionably
render service to the community before they idly consume services. Mr. Loch quotes former Poor Law
Committee-men as pointing out that certain forms of
poor relief are "premiums upon indolence and vice."
If there be any meaning in words, our systems of
land accumulation and free bequest of money-capital
are premiums upon indolence and vice, fostering both
in the highest degree; yet it never occurs to the
critics in question to say so. On the other hand, the
relatively much smaller risk of promoting indolence
and vice by a national pension system can be guarded
against, and will be increasingly so in practice, by
public interest inspiring public criticism.

Mr. Loch's general objection to a national pension

system, then, breaks down alike morally and economically, he having, indeed, no economic light on the subject at all. But there is a general objection which he might very well have made—that, namely, which has been above indicated in connecting the pension scheme with the population problem. The omission all round to raise the population difficulty is at least a proof of the falsity of the common assertion that that principle is usually employed as a means of rebutting proposals made in the interests of the people. I do not here employ it with any such purpose. Rather I bring it forward in the belief that the growing acceptance of the pension principle will be the most effective means of bringing home the population principle to the general intelligence. Those who have hitherto refused to face it must then do so. Any measure of systematic State provision for the necessities of the people will constitute a clear national risk, unless at the same time the need for limitation of rate of increase is generally recognised. Of late years there has been an economic conspiracy of silence, or worse, on the subject; and even enlightened writers like Professor Marshall and Professor Sidgwick either obscure the issue or deny the solution. In his latest work Professor Sidgwick makes the astonishing declaration that in the present state of civilisation he considers the increase of human life "in the world" as a good and not as an evil.[1] Since he at the same time admits that some day it is likely to be necessary to restrict population, he is committed, in the very act of encouraging increase, to the view that such increase

---

[1] *Elements of Politics,* p. 301.

tends to become a danger. That is to say, the position
of civilisation is going to get worse and not better.
Yet it lies on the face of the case that such worsen-
ment can only appear under the guise of poverty
and struggle for subsistence, phenomena which are
glaringly apparent in the present state of civilisation,
in which Professor Sidgwick thinks all increase of
population is a good.

The fact is, it appears, that Professor Sidgwick
makes the ordinary empiric's confusion between *gross*
and *net* increase of population. He has not realised
that a restriction of *gross* increase of population is
compatible with a continued *net* increase of population, in respect that of the fewer children born a
larger proportion can subsist. This lesson is of the
very essence of the Neo-Malthusian doctrine. [1] But
even if we consider the demand for a continued net
increase of population, it is plain that it rests, even
when put forward by a thinker like Professor Sidgwick, on no scientific estimate of good and evil. The
first condition of such an estimate is a discrimination of
the various lots into which human beings are born ;
but Mr. Sidgwick makes no discrimination whatever.
Thus can sociology still be written.

IV.

But, even assuming a recognition of the law of
population, there is still our problem of consumption,
which the advocates of State pensions leave wholly

---

[1] See the author's pamphlet on *Over-Population* (Forder,
Stonecutter Street).

out of account, framing as they do a sociological proposition without a study of the economic contingencies.
With or without limitation of families, we saw, the
principle of parsimony would lead to economic over-
production of easily produced necessaries, and the
principle of parsimony, unless discredited or effectively
thwarted, would continue to operate widely even
alongside of a State pension system. Even if pensions
be withheld from all who have investments—and that
is a point that must clearly be considered when we
come to details—those who do the bulk of the present
"saving" would continue to do so, and the kind of
consumption possible to the pensioners, at the rates of
pension thus far proposed, would certainly not permit of any great raising of the standard of consumption. So the industrial problem would still subsist,
and we should soon be led up to the question of doles
to the unemployed.

Now, no State could enter on a system of doles to
the unemployed without rapid demoralisation and no
less rapid impoverishment. The causes which created
the lack of employment would subsist under a system
of doles. Rapidly perishable forms of wealth would
be freely produced at demand, and still there would be
idleness, unless among the classes with most purchasing
power there arose an increasing demand for the higher
and less easily producible forms of wealth—for
artistic products, in short. And what present likeli-
hood is there of these classes thus raising their
standards of consumption while they have no other
means than saving and investment of securing for their
old age the measure of income that investments might

yield them ? Plainly, the establishment of pensions for
the workers is only one side of the process of reconstruction ; and we must try to ascertain how the rest
of the process should go.

First, we come back to the old principle, otherwise
arrived at,[1] of a graduated income tax as a necessary
means towards the payment of the National Debt.
Here we have at once a means of rectifying plain
political injustice and of checking under-consumption,
provided, that is, that we specially tax idle income
from investments. This is the course prescribed by
political equity apart from economic sociology, and it
entirely consists also with the economico-sociological
prescription. But the taxation of incomes will at first
necessarily tend to make those taxed spend less on
consumption ; and here, as before, we are faced by the
need for special employment of labour. Such employment can only be supplied by public action ; and I can
suggest no better lines of such action than genuine
public works, such as corporate cultivation of waste
or withheld lands ; the scientific utilisation of sewage and consequent salvation of rivers ; the proper
tunnelling of streets for sewage and lighting purposes,
and the rebuilding of the worst parts of our cities, including in that the erection of good dwellings and
noble public buildings.

Thus far we shall provide for the employment of
unskilled and partially skilled labour generally ; and
if at the same time we establish a pension system for
the workers, stipulating that there shall be propor-
tional deduction where the pensioner has other sources

---

[1] See *Modern Humanists*, Epilogue.

of income, we may take it that common consumption will be fairly safe. All this, be it observed, comes far short of the universal transformation demanded by the neck-or-nothing Socialists, who propose the nationalisation of all means of production. That is a transformation which human nature cannot accomplish save by a prolonged course of gradual change : what we are here proposing is a set of social departures plainly required by the industrial and moral situation, and as plainly practicable. The reform of taxation, of course, goes upon a principle which equally prescribes the nationalisation, as is found feasible, of monopoly-sources of profit, such as railways, gas-works, water-works, and banks. Merely to nationalise these, and to secure the national utilisation of the land, will be hard enough work for some generations to come ; and it is needless here to anticipate the problems of further nationalisation of sources of profit which will arise when these have been grappled with. Suffice it to say that by all these means the sources of idle living may be gradually restricted without any harm to industry generally, and even without any violent hardship to the idle classes, which will be gradually eliminated. The practice of saving will be continued by the non-pensioned classes on their own behalf ; but when en-lightened consumption is more and more generally recognised as the right economic and social course, there will be a decline in the desire to endow idle families—provided only that there are careers open which shall yield young people fair chances of living in return for services rendered to society.

And here arises the question whether an extending

pension system (for I will assume that as the community is found to prosper on the new lines, pensions
will be raised to the workers generally) may alone be
trusted to secure such raising of the standards of consumption as shall elicit in an ever-increasing degree
the higher kinds of service, and not merely increase
the run upon the lower. We have seen that
machinery will always easily overtake the demand
for most necessaries (though the limits of the food
and fuel supplies, not to speak of room for houses
and gardens, must always be less elastic); and that
the true cure for over-supply of labour is primarily
restraint of population, and secondarily demand for
artistic products. Given the recognition of these
principles, will the pension system, with its security
of life, suffice to make them work ? Will the classes
employed and pensioned by the State be safe to provide as well among them for the maintenance of
literature, art, and science, as society does at present ?

I would answer that, without any such premature
extension of public employment as would be a social
danger comparable to the present moral evil of a
large class of idle rich, the public service will necessarily tend to provide more and more for the fostering
of the higher standards of consumption alongside of
the raising of the standards of the workers. The
education system must clearly be improved, till the
higher grades are relatively as fully available in the
public interest as the lower. And as the official
pension system is already in force in the public
service generally, and is bound to be extended rather
than dropped, it will come about that the great class

engaged in all kinds of teaching, like the other classes
of public servants (likely ere long to include, as before
noted, the employees on the railway and gas and
water systems), will be in a good position to consume
the higher forms of literary and artistic service,
leaving the supply of these services (as apart from
public teaching) to the free operation of the present
supply-forces. In this, as in commercial matters,
there need be no fear of lack of supply, if there is
demand. And on the lines specified, demand will,
I think, be forthcoming. Indeed, it is safe to say
that on such lines of evolution, demand for the higher
intellectual services will be relatively much larger
than it is at present. It is one of the darkest features
of the present system that the ideals or standards of
consumption on the intellectual side rise so slowly, nay,
even seem at points to sink relatively to the material
possibilities. So far from there being, as Cairnes
implied, a danger that the more a State is socialised
the greater will be the risk of a decline of the arts
and sciences, it is inconceivable that any State more
socialised than ours should in future provide worse
for the advancement of these than we are doing at
present.[1]

Throughout all this argument, be it remembered,
there is assumed the general practice of restraint of

---

[1] The prospects of literature under a more socialised system
have, I think, been even under-estimated from a professedly socialist point of view, while those of art and science have not been
clearly enough set forth. See the articles on "Art and Literature under Socialism" in the *New Review* for January, 1891,
by Messrs. Morris & Salt.

births. Needless to say, this must hold good for the more cultured as well as for the less; and this restraint alone will serve to improve the situation for the "upper" (there will still in a sense be upper and lower, or more and less cultured) as well as for the "lower" classes. At present the pressure of the competitive saving system is much intensified by the high rate of increase among the middle-classes, for fathers naturally want to provide for their daughters, and to start their sons in life with "capital." When the English middle-classes learn the lesson of rationalism in life, the ideal of endowed idleness will be the more easily superseded because the opportunities of worthy and refined employment will be proportionally much greater as the number of helpless middle-class scions of both sexes relatively falls off. Thus in time may be attained the complete euthanasia or elimination of that grave social evil, the idle class; the community safeguarding otherwise, step by step, all the compensations which the existence of that class has hitherto involved. Of course the complete elimination will mean the socialisation of all the present sources of interest on invested money-credit.

V.

But already we have gone, for scientific purposes, quite far enough in anticipation of future possibilities; and our exposition must end on the strictly practical plane of present day economics. The practical doctrine of this second part of our inquiry, over and above restraint of population, is summed up in (1) reform of taxation to the primary end of paying off the National Debt; (2) public works, to employ the labour that tends to be thrown idle as a result of the liquidation of the Debt; (3) a national system of pensions. The last point to be considered is the method of the pension system in the light of the economic principles before established.

It speedily appears that the old idea of a National Insurance Fund is out of the question. Even apart from any perception of the general Fallacy of Saving, it is widely admitted that such a fund would be unworkable. It is hard enough for private Insurance Companies to go on investing their funds profitably, without the Government attempting to compete with them as an investor on a gigantic scale. But further, it is being widely recognised that the collection of premiums, or specific payments towards pensions, would be an enormously difficult matter; and already, alongside of the schemes which specify such charges and payments, there are others which frankly propose to make a national pension charge without exacting payments from individual workers. Such are the proposals of Mr. R. P. Hardy [1] and Dr. Hunter.[2]

Here, however, there is a risk of such misconception as is set up by the phrase "free education." Indeed, there being a specific education-rate, the risk of misconception is greater. At the present moment, the working-classes pay, relatively to their mere money income, a very large proportion of the national taxa-

---

[1] Pamphlet on *Old Age Pensions* (Knight & Co., 1891).
[2] Articles in *Weekly Dispatch*.

tion, of which so great a mass goes to pay interest on national debt. Even if they were not thus taxed in respect of their consumption, they obviously contribute the great mass of the really useful services by which all incomes are built up; but as a matter of fact they positively pay out of their wages a large part of the national revenue. A sound system of taxation would remove much of their present burden, by making an end of the taxes on articles of food. But if a pension system can be established, it may be on many grounds expedient to impose a direct income-tax on the working as on other classes. Such a tax would represent their specific contribution to the national burdens, and would constitute by far the best *quid pro quo* as against their pensions. It would be a universal tax as against a universal obligation ; and it would be impossible even for empirics then to speak as if the workers drew pensions without doing anything to pay them. No doubt there would still be outcry on the part of the monied classes. So deeply rooted is the notion that labour subsists chiefly by the bounty of capitalists, that in the recent case of the Scotch railway strike Mr. Lang, strong in intuitive sociology, could come forward to satirise those who sympathised with the strikers, as being generous at the expense of the shareholders. It did not occur to Mr. Lang that to sympathise with the shareholders was to be generous at the expense of the men, whose lives were spent in earning dividends for the shareholders. But while Mr. Lang's view will of course be popular among shareholders, we may hope that even in that class there are now many who deriving their sociology from other than belletrist sources, can see that it is industry which pays dividends, and not dividends that pay industry.

That the workers would themselves readily acquiesce in such a course seems the more likely in view of the favour with which the Bismarckian system of national insurance is regarded by them in Germany, where the workmen's contribution is exacted through the employer. That in itself seems a cumbrous and vexatious course under any circumstances, and would certainly not be easy of introduction in England. But inasmuch as the workers pay educational and other rates already, there need be little difficulty in charging them with a national rate, which it would be so clearly worth their while to pay, and which moreover ought to be a less burden than that which at present presses on them in respect of the taxes on their food and their poor " luxuries."

The great matter is that there shall be a general abandonment of the established delusion that the universal saving of sums of money-credit, as an outcome of non-consumption of the products of industry, can ever lead to all-round well-being. And therefore it is that I have stipulated for the limitation of the pension in cases where the pensioner has an income from invested savings. It must be admitted, however, that this stipulation can hardly be insisted on so long as the pension paid is only a few shillings a week, as is at present proposed. The question, therefore, need not be politically argued on this line at present. It will properly arise first in connection with those official pensions which are sufficient in themselves to

K

sustain life in comfort. These are as yet mainly restricted to the upper grades of the public service ; and
to raise the principle in that direction will doubtless
give much offence at the outset. But if there be any
validity in the foregoing economic analysis, raised the
question must be ere very long. And we may hope
that the natural tendency to increase the small pensions
first asked for will be a force which will necessitate
the reconsideration of the received economic doctrine.
Legislators will never agree to a national system of
comfort-giving pensions while the theory of saving
holds its ground. That theory rests, as we have seen,
on unenlightened self-interest. But inasmuch as a
system of comfort-giving pensions would coincide
with the impulse of economically enlightened self-
interest, it seems reasonable to conclude that, once
established in a democratic State, it will be so developed as to undermine or override the contrary
policy, which will, besides, be scientifically discredited
step for step with the successful working of the
rational regimen of advancing consumption.

THE END.

Printed by Cowan & Co., Limited, Perth.

INDEX.

SOCIAL SCIENCE SERIES.

SCARLET CLOTH, EACH 2s. 6d.

SOCIAL SCIENCE SERIES—(Continued).

20. Common Sense about Women.   T. W. HIGGINSON.
"An admirable collection of papers, advocating in the most liberal spirit the emancipation of women."—*Woman's Herald.*

21. The Unearned Increment.   W. H. DAWSON.
"A concise but comprehensive volume."—*Echo.*

22. Our Destiny.   LAURENCE GRONLUND.
"A very vigorous little book, dealing with the influence of Socialism on morals and religion."—*Daily Chronicle.*

23. The Working-Class Movement in America.
Dr. EDWARD and E. MARX AVELING.
"Will give a good idea of the condition of the working classes in America, and of the various organisations which they have formed."—*Scots Leader.*

24. Luxury.   Prof. EMILE DE LAVELEYE.
"An eloquent plea on moral and economical grounds for simplicity of life."—*Academy.*

25. The Land and the Labourers.   Rev. C. W. STUBBS, M.A.
"This admirable book should be circulated in every village in the country."—*Manchester Guardian.*

26. The Evolution of Property.   PAUL LAFARGUE.
"Will prove interesting and profitable to all students of economic history."—*Scotsman.*

27. Crime and its Causes.   W. DOUGLAS MORRISON.
"Can hardly fail to suggest to all readers several new and pregnant reflections on the subject."—*Anti-Jacobin.*

28. Principles of State Interference.   D. G. RITCHIE, M.A.
"An interesting contribution to the controversy on the functions of the State."—*Glasgow Herald.*

29. German Socialism and F. Lassalle.   W. H. DAWSON.
"As a biographical history of German Socialistic movements during this century it may be accepted as complete."—*British Weekly.*

30. The Purse and the Conscience.   H. M. THOMPSON, B.A. (Cantab.).
"Shows common sense and fairness in his arguments."—*Scotsman.*

31. Origin of Property in Land.   FUSTEL DE COULANGES. Edited, with an Introductory Chapter on the English Manor, by Prof. W. J. ASHLEY, M.A.
"His views are clearly stated, and are worth reading."—*Saturday Review.*

32. The English Republic.   W. J. LINTON. Edited by KINETON PARKES.
"Characterised by that vigorous intellectuality which has marked his long life of literary and artistic activity."—*Glasgow Herald.*

33. The Co-Operative Movement.   BEATRICE POTTER.
"Without doubt the ablest and most philosophical analysis of the Co-Operative Movement which has yet been produced."—*Speaker.*

34. Neighbourhood Guilds.   Dr. STANTON COIT.
"A most suggestive little book to anyone interested in the social question."—*Pall Mall Gazette.*

35. Modern Humanists.   J. M. ROBERTSON.
"Mr. Robertson's style is excellent—nay, even brilliant—and his purely literary criticisms bear the mark of much acumen."—*Times.*

36. Outlooks from the New Standpoint.   E. BELFORT BAX.
"Mr. Bax is a very acute and accomplished student of history and economics."—*Daily Chronicle.*

37. Distributing Co-Operative Societies.   Dr. LUIGI PIZZAMIGLIO. Edited by F. J. SNELL.
"Dr. Pizzamiglio has gathered together and grouped a wide array of facts and statistics, and they speak for themselves."—*Speaker.*

38. Collectivism and Socialism.   By A. NACQUET. Edited by W. HEAFORD.
"An admirable criticism by a well-known French politician of the New Socialism of Marx and Lassalle."—*Daily Chronicle.*

SOCIAL SCIENCE SERIES—(Continued).

SOCIAL SCIENCE SERIES—(Continued).

SWAN SONNENSCHEIN & CO., Lim., LONDON.

NEW YORK: CHARLES SCRIBNER'S SONS.